SELF
CREATION

SELF CREATION

DR. GEORGE WEINBERG

ST. MARTIN'S PRESS
NEW YORK

Library of Congress Cataloging in Publication Data

Weinberg, George H.
  Self creation.

  1. Self-actualization (Psychology).   I. Title.
BF637.S8W348   158'.1   77-10375

ISBN 0-312-71232-4

Thanks to Tom McCormack, president of St. Martin's, for his personal involvement with this book at every stage—and for his contributions to it over a period of years; and to Hope Dellon, who has been innovative and creative in the editing. Also to Alice Fennessey, Louis R. Ormont, C. A. Tripp, Barbara Warren, and Steve Yates for their psychological insights.

CONTENTS

SELF
CREATION

"WHY AM I LIKE THIS?" 1

"Why am I like this?" This question, sometimes asked in public, more often in solitude, and almost always in anguish, is asked by absolutely everyone at some time.

Behind it lies another question, less often explicitly put: "Is it possible to change?" Or sometimes: "Can I change myself?" Or even: "Can *you* change me?"

The answer to that last question is No. No one else can change you. But the answer to the second question is Yes. You *can* change yourself. This book will tell you how.

The book will make some very large claims. To convey its message as clearly and urgently as possible, it will say things in broad absolutes and it will simplify—in fact, oversimplify—as an anatomist might who starts his course by saying, "The human body is 'only' a system of pulleys and hinges arranged on a frame called the skeleton."

To that end, I should start now by saying that this book will make "only" one claim, but it's almost as large a claim as I can imagine: *This book will help you to see what you are, how you became the way you are, and how to change the way you are.* But, for all its aspirations, this book cannot change you.

Only you can change you. Because only you created you.

What the book *can* do is help you to change yourself. By explaining precisely how you created—and are constantly re-creating—yourself.

Not theological or biological creation, but psychological. All the feelings, attitudes, and beliefs that make up your personality are created, caused by, you. Moreover, by your voluntary, controllable actions. You can, and do, form and re-form your own personality. Every day.

"But I don't want to change my whole personality—just this particular aspect of it!" Agreed—though you may find that one aspect involves other aspects in a surprising way. The principle of change explained in these pages allows us to focus where we want. You're anxious about this feeling, that attitude, or this belief: In all likelihood you can change it. Because it's you who built it up, you who are keeping it there, and you who can take it down.

We can reframe the book's "only" claim. There is a principle—almost as mechanically dependable and predictable as a typewriter—hit this key, and that mark will appear —that links your own voluntary actions with the feelings, attitudes, and beliefs that follow the actions. Notice I say "follow." Not "precede." Everyone observes the link the other way round. *Because* I feel this, I *do* that.

This book is going to reverse that sequence. It will say, "*Because* I do that, I *feel* this." But in a very special way. You might say, "That's no news. Sure, feelings *follow* actions. I already know that because I did such-and-such I now feel guilty."

That's the sequence. But it's not the causal connection I mean. Guilt is an effect that comes from *reflection* about what you did. The effect I'll talk about is *direct*, following inexorably from the fact that you chose the action regardless of whether you reflected on it. These direct effects are the most important there are in the formation of your psyche—and yet you may never have dreamed they exist.

The effect is absolutely dependable. It is ironclad, undodgeable, unfailing: *Every* time you do this (for such-

and-such a reason), you will feel that. This means you are always rewarded for beneficial choices, always penalized for harmful ones. Because there is a basic law of human nature constantly at work, a law that is universal and yet so elusive that it has escaped all our predecessors who have been asking "Why am I like this?" for generations.

One shortcoming in saying "I feel guilty because I did that" is that it does not explain *why* doing that made you feel guilty—or anxious, or depressed, or angry, or unloved, or whatever. "But I feel guilty about that because I was taught as a child it was bad and I believe it still." Why do you believe it still? Certainly you don't still believe all the things taught you as a child. This book will explain why you still believe it, and how to stop believing it—if you want to.

It will explain why you now have every feeling and attitude you do, and it will provide the key to changing them. It will explain this not historically, in the sense of citing the specific first lesson you received. I don't know your biography. But I do know the basic principle at work. To change a current feeling, you don't need to know how it originally arose—though it would be interesting—any more than, to deflect an avalanche, you need to know which was the first pebble to fall.

In an avalanche, it's what's happening here and now that counts. And in your personality, it's what you're doing here and now that counts.

This is directly contrary to the tenets of traditional analysis. Given the unsuccessful record of traditional analysis as a treatment and given its inability to predict, which means a fundamental inability to explain or to be tested, it is justifiably a receding tide in psychotherapy. Many analysts today are relieved to see it go. It was devised out of immense good will, but so was the bleeding of fevered patients centuries ago. So it is going, and it should go.

To be replaced by what? By a theory that can explain, can predict, can be tested. And has, in the hands of the increasing number of therapists using it, a good record of success.

Having mentioned therapists, I should quickly add this: The method of self-change that I'll describe can be understood and carried out by you alone. It does not require an analyst. You don't need one. An analyst who practices with this method might speed your insights, but he won't discover anything you can't discover on your own. In the end, the analyst is like this book. He can help you to change, but he can't change you. Only you can do that.

If the claim this book makes is true—that it will explain the simple fundamental principle behind the formation and re-formation of all your feelings, attitudes, and beliefs —it could have, and I fervently hope does have, the most important impact on your life of any single book you'll ever read. Consider this: if only one-tenth of what it asserts is true, it can still change your life.

Now, on to the Principle.

SELF CREATION 2

This is the basic principle at work every day of your life behind the creation of your personality:

EVERY TIME YOU ACT, YOU ADD STRENGTH TO THE MOTIVATING IDEA BEHIND WHAT YOU'VE DONE.

It sounds too simple to explain so much, but it's not. There are other ways of phrasing this, and I'll give several, but none of them should sound more complicated than this one. The Principle is true, it accounts for the entire treasury of feelings, attitudes, and beliefs that comprise your personality, and I won't make it truer by making it sound more complex. The task at hand is to make clear what it *means*—and what it *implies*.

Let me restate it.

Every time you do something, the motivating idea or feeling that prompted you to do it is intensified. It can be an idea about yourself, about others, about the world. Whatever it is, it's reinforced when you act on it.

It's as though the act retypes the motivating message in your mind. When it's not acted on, the message becomes weaker, as if fading from an electronic screen. When it *is* acted on, it becomes brighter, louder, recharged, prompting still more of the same acts.

The sheer fact of acting on any belief or feeling makes you believe or feel it more.

It takes some time to understand the Principle, to *see* that it works, and how useful it is. There are factors that obscure it in action, and we'll examine those. Perhaps the most important is that often we don't recognize the motivating idea behind our acts, so we don't make the connection between the motive, the act, and the intensification of the motive. One of the tasks of this book will be to help you identify just what is behind many of your actions.

Now let me ask you to do something. Over the succeeding pages, please try to *hunt out what is true* about this Principle and my claims for it. There will still be plenty of time to criticize it, to find exceptions. But don't do that at the outset.

My reason for asking stems directly from the Principle itself. Indeed, it illustrates the Principle. It says, if you now bend yourself to trying to prove the book wrong, the more you bend, the more determined you will be that it *is* wrong—regardless of the evidence.

Haven't you seen this happen many times in your life? At a party, Ralph makes an offhand remark critical of a certain movie. When he first makes his remark, his attitude toward the movie is actually mild—he might even have liked it on the whole—and his remark is merely to display his cleverness. But he gets a surprise. Instead of just smiling at the gibe, someone at the party contradicts it. Ralph answers back. The other man rebuts again. Ralph attacks another aspect of the movie. The man is unmoved. Ralph tears into the whole movie, the director's entire opus, and the other man's notorious bad taste. In a half-hour, Ralph's basic attitude toward the movie has changed. Now he really hates it. At the next party he goes to, almost the first subject he brings up will be the movie, to attack it thoroughly.

What is happening here? Many things. But, for now, I want to focus on only one. It is the Principle at work. Every time Ralph speaks to criticize the movie, one motivation behind his act is a belief that the movie is flawed— and this belief is reinforced, strengthened, by his choice to act on it.

And this is *always* the case: act on a feeling, attitude, or belief, and you reinforce that belief. Ralph was creating his own feelings. By his own actions.

Let's say that someone Ralph respects points out an aspect of what happened. Says: "When you started out, you didn't really dislike the movie, but at the end you hated it." And let's say Ralph even concedes this. It's unlikely he'd see why. He'd say, "Once I thought about it, I saw how rotten it was." And if he's psychologistic he might add, "The guy made me mad and I probably transferred my anger to the movie."

But that wouldn't be it. Suppose he had been *defending* the movie and the other man made him angry. He wouldn't end up hating the movie. Just the opposite. His angry acts in defense of the movie would have made him even more convinced of its worthiness.

Again—always—he would have been molding his own feelings by his acts. And always in accordance with the Principle.

Let's go now to what motivated Ralph to make his would-be clever remark in the first place. Because whatever that motivation was, it was intensified in the next half-hour.

Ralph was anxious about his reputation for intellect. He grew up in a home where the number one virtue was brains. His father gave quizzes at the dinner table. If one of the children didn't know the answer he was fair game for ridicule. Ralph was not athletic or good-looking, and he had no humor; he got his praise by being smart. He took this lesson outside the home and became a triumphant student. He was convinced his only claim to admiration was his intelligence, so he displayed it every chance he got. The more he acted on this premise—that brains were his only attribute—the more convinced he became of it. Often it worked against him more than for him: in college he was known as The Great Contradictor.

So, at the party Ralph was just doing what he'd done for years. His initial remark was meant only to show his cleverness. When he was contradicted, he lashed back not primarily out of any great disdain for the movie, but to preserve his only claim to merit. If someone proves that Ralph's brain is defective, where does that leave Ralph? Desperate. Clawing for survival.

How should we express his motivation? Like this: He was acting on the belief that his only claim to acceptance was intellect, and that, stripped of his right to that claim, he would be nothing, pitied, despised, totally without attraction. *And with every further word of argument he reinforced this belief.*

So the movie is the first thing he brings up at the next party. He's made himself anxious, and he longs avidly for another chance to prove himself. Not just to the gathering, but to himself. He must win tonight the argument he fears he lost last night.

But notice: He is again acting on the belief that intellect is everything, and even if he wins the new argument hands down, he will still be reinstating in his mind the conviction that intellect is everything.

How many times have we seen people "carrying on" and known instinctively that if only we could get them to slow down—to curtail what they were doing—they'd stop building their anxiety, or hatred, or even their misplaced high hopes? Why? Not just because they were "keeping the adrenaline flowing." Because in some way we knew they were *convincing themselves.* By their very actions.

That's what this book is about. It says that this Principle, which we've all recognized at work some time, is at work *all* the time, and that its influence on our personality is much more basic and continuous than ever before realized.

Suppose Ralph had one more motivating element working within him. The man who contradicts him is not entirely unknown to him, and Ralph doesn't like him much. Let's not even posit a reason why; he just doesn't like him. His dislike is mild, but it's enough to make him seize on an opportunity to put the man in his place. And that's part of why he lashes back so vigorously. With every counterattack he mounts, he's acting on what we can call the *premise* of his dislike. And thus the dislike is increased more and more. By the end of the night he despises the man . . . as much as the movie.

Through the ages writers have remarked on this one way or another: Do a man a bad turn, and you will find it hard to forgive him. Attack a man and he comes to seem worthy of attack. If you want your G.I.'s to hate the Japanese enough to kill them, don't just tell atrocity stories; paint Japanese faces on the bayonet practice dummies and have them stab. The very action will generate savagery. The greatest propagandists in history have known this essential truth which springs directly from the Principle: If you want to build dedication to the "movement" in your followers, don't just preach your text, however true. Get them to *do* something. Something based on a belief in the movement. That's how you inculcate belief.

This touches on a discomforting point. The Principle has the potential to be used by demagogues and manipulators.

But though the Principle has been used that way, remember that the individual does the choosing. Society invites the individual to act. But each person creates—and sustains—his own outlook. If you understand the Principle, you're less likely to fall victim to such manipulators.

The Principle explains why some people harbor what the rest of us consider totally irrational convictions. Even the most reasonable person can come to believe highly irrational things—can convince himself of their truth by certain actions. Take the severely paranoid person. You look at him and shake your head. You're almost prompted to dismiss him as insane. Because he has such wild fears about what is going to befall him. "How could he believe such things?" Yes, how? Not by an examination of the logical evidence that might support his bizarre beliefs. It's not *evidence* that is making him believe what he does.

As a final, lighter example in this chapter, aimed at illustrating the Principle, turn to the nineteenth-century French play *Le Voyage de Monsieur Perrichon*. Perrichon is rich, and he has a daughter. Daniel and Armand seek her hand in marriage. They know the choice will be made by Perrichon, so they court his approval. Armand's strategy is to do what he can for Perrichon. Daniel's is to get Perrichon *to do things for him*. He arranges a series of plights for himself from which, by certain actions, Perrichon can save him. His final coup is to pretend to be stuck in a crevice on Mont Blanc freezing to death. Perrichon struggles to rescue him, and with each new effort his determination to save that worthy boy increases. He succeeds in the apparent rescue and, hugging the estimable lad to his bosom, he chooses him for his daughter. Just in time Perrichon overhears Daniel gloating about his strategy, and the old man gives his daughter to the right man after all.

Manipulation? Yes. But where Daniel merely entices Perrichon to act in a certain way, it is Perrichon who manipulates Perrichon's feelings. Daniel understood the Principle. If Perrichon had too, he never would have come so close to making a tragic mistake.

And that's true of all of us. An understanding of how the Principle works in our lives—which the rest of the book will try to make clear—is bound to help us protect ourselves. Protect ourselves against unwanted change or against unwanted *sameness*. I want to call the fruit of the Principle self-control. Or, better, self-liberation. Or, best, Self Creation.

OURS IS TO REASON WHY? 3

There are several questions about the Principle that often arise very early. Addressing them here and in the next chapter can help make the Principle clearer.

The first is: "The Principle may have truth in it, but can it be as fundamental as you say and still have escaped the perception of professional psychotherapists for so long?" Yes, it can. There have been professional psychologists in the modern sense for less than a hundred years. Still, one of the earliest psychologists and one of the greatest—William James—came close to uncovering the Principle. He (with C. J. Lange) argued that certain emotions *follow* the action instead of vice versa. We are frightened because we run. Eventually this led James to a kind of action therapy: Do this, and you feel that. "In order to feel kindly toward a person to whom we have been inimical, the only way is more or less deliberately to smile, to make sympathetic inquiries, and to force ourselves to say genial things."

But this doesn't often work. Why? James didn't know. So this method—which is sometimes termed behavioral modification therapy—did not catch on around the turn of the century.

Eventually, another therapy, soon to be called psychoanalysis, gained ascendancy. In essence it was just the opposite of behavior modification. Freud's attention was held by his observation that people just don't seem to change. Nothing a patient did mattered. He could move halfway around the globe, change jobs, marry a different woman—he'd still be the same underneath. James's advice—act differently and you'll feel different—was absurd. It didn't work. Because it was superficial. The problem, Freud felt, was deep down and far back. We must dig for it.

The only problem was that Freud's therapy didn't work either, and, toward the end of his life, in "Analysis Terminable and Interminable," he began to despair about the possibility of change in the psyche.

Eventually, younger therapists who had been schooled in the tradition of Freud began to drift, occasionally, toward encouraging their patients to modify their behavior in certain ways. But the aim was still narrow, often devised to improve the patient's "self-image" by, say, improving what others thought of him. "Stop contradicting so much," they might have told Ralph, "because it makes people dislike you and you see it in their faces and that fills you with self-loathing." This advice has some merit (and some drawbacks), but it is incomplete.

Now we can see what happened. James was on the right path, but he didn't get there. Then came Freud, with a thousand valuable observations of human behavior. But just as a great philosopher like Aristotle could lead later thinkers down a long wrong path, so did Freud, by certain assumptions. He assumed that you have to change inside before you can act in a healthy way. And that you've got to understand your childhood, how you became as you are, before you can solve a problem. Both assumptions were false, and they took us away from the right path.

Well, what was wrong with James's theory? And with the behavior modification theory of recent times? Just this: they did not perceive the role of motivation. They did not see that it is the premise behind the act that is reinstated, reinforced, strengthened, when we act.

All of us have "tried to like" someone at some time. We are congenial. We still don't like him. We end up feeling disturbed and frustrated—filled with an increased desire that we perceive will be thwarted. At last we throw up our hands. "To hell with him. I just can't like him. God knows I tried." So we cease trying. And promptly even the desire to like him wanes. Because we are no longer continually reinstating the desire by actions stemming from the desire.

Of course, as James must have observed, sometimes when we make an effort to like someone, we do end up liking him. How's that? Many possible reasons. Very likely our friendly attitude gets perceived by John and he begins to open himself up in a way he never has before. He reveals some unexpected aspect that we do like. The aspect pleases us enough so that we make a sincerely genial gesture—we say or do something motivated by our liking—and, bang! our liking starts to build. The Principle at work.

James knew there was a connection between actions and subsequent feelings, but he mistook what the connection was. Before moving into psychology, James was a medical doctor who taught anatomy at Harvard. His original idea about action causing emotion was based on his studies of physiology. We run: this stimulates glands, they stimulate emotion. The action causes the emotion. But this focus kept him from shifting his eyes back to where the *motivation* lay brooding, unnoticed, and holding within it the whole answer.

Another possible reason why James missed the connection is one that is still with us: the two-stage effect of any act. The *immediate* effect of any act is to satisfy, assuage, reduce the motivating impulse behind it. But the ultimate effect is to strengthen it. This is most keenly observable with a habit. You feel the impulse to indulge it. If you do, the impulse is reduced, even eliminated—

temporarily. But the very fact of acting on it has ultimately reinforced it.

Picture a habit as our whole life-style in microcosm. Whatever impulses we act on are entrenched by the act. Ultimately. The first stage may appear to be a reduction, but this only serves to obscure the lasting effect. The paranoid who checks and rechecks his locks feels first-stage relief—and ultimate reinforcement of his paranoia.

HAVE YOURSELF A HAPPY TRAUMA 4

The second question often asked is this: "How can the Principle account for the consistency of a person's personality?" The Principle says that people are, in effect, reinstating their personality every day. If you don't act on a motivating feeling, it wanes and dies. Evidently you need to perform regularly a whole set of actions based on your feelings, attitudes, and beliefs. Otherwise, the Principle seems to be saying, your personality will constantly drift, shift, and alter—because these feelings need the regular recharging they get from being acted on. As Freud made evident, we don't just change automatically. We have all noticed how consistent people are in their attitudes going back to their childhood. If we're really re-creating ourselves every day, how do we explain this consistency?

It is true that many people's personalities show consistency throughout their lives. But there are also people who do change, long after childhood, all by themselves. They change for the better—and they change for the worse. There are people who, persevering on their own—without ever having seen an analyst, depth or otherwise—have overcome every conceivable kind of psychological problem, regardless of age.

At least one despairing study has reported that the percentage of patients whom psychotherapy helped to leave a mental hospital was no greater than those who recovered spontaneously. Psychotherapy usually does help people somewhat. But certain kinds of treatment actually militate against change—because they require that the patient make no drastic changes in his life-style during therapy.

People do change all on their own. Classical therapy has recognized this too and has expressed it in certain theories of "trauma." A trauma, traditionally, is some dire event that does grave and lasting harm to the psyche. Indeed, the word *trauma* in Greek means *wound*. But this, I think, is an unfortunate derivation. Because not all traumas—in the sense of events that cause changes in psychic life-style—are bad. Some are distinctly fortunate, the luckiest thing that ever happened to the "wounded" one.

The Principle accounts for traumas in a much more complete way than earlier theories. More interestingly, it accounts for why traumas *don't* occur, too.

Consider, a mini-trauma that we all have heard about: being thrown from a horse. Received wisdom says get right back on. Why? "Because you're apt to lose your confidence if you don't." Why? "Well, because . . . you'll brood about it?"

The Principle explains why explicitly. Any acts of avoidance based on fear will entrench the fear. This practice, though not the Principle, is recognized throughout life. Performers of every kind sense its importance. Race-car drivers force themselves to drive again as soon as possible after an accident because otherwise they foresee losing their nerve.

Don't let a momentary failure be followed by a lifetime of fear. Notice I say the failure is *followed by* the permanent fear. I don't want to say the failure *causes* it. This would obscure the real causation: It's the *avoidance* that causes the fear. Everybody who fails does not then fear. Everybody who avoids *does* then fear.

Now consider a more important trauma. Louise was fourteen, just at the age when she was beginning to accept herself as a sexual person, when she was raped. The event itself was battering, but over quickly. What followed was not over quickly. Her first reaction was shame, and this was heightened by her father's accusation that she had enticed the man. In her mortification she let the event prompt her to terminate all activities with sexual over-tones, however mild. She stopped her dancing lessons, changed her way of dressing to ultraconservative, sought out only prim friends, avoided boys. Her whole mode of life became one of avoiding sex, condemning it, creating shame, a suspicion of men, and a loathing of her own body and its sexual inclinations. And with each passing year she entrenched her fear and loathing.

First, notice the awful timing of the rape. She was at an age when her sexual mode was most vulnerable. Had the rape occurred much later, when she had a fully established sexual life-style, the chances of her changing that style overnight would have been much less. And if she had been raped much earlier, when she had no sexual life-style available to her—an eight-year-old would find it difficult to adopt a style of avoiding sexual encounters—the chances of a permanent trauma occurring would again have been less. But Louise's sex life was, at fourteen, a budding branch that she could bend and redirect forever after.

If Louise's parents had worked hard at *discouraging changes of behavior* in reaction to the rape, they would have helped her a great deal. Suppose they had insisted she go on with her dance lessons and remain in the school play. Suppose they had gone out and bought her more dresses of the kind she was beginning to admire. At the outset, still distressed, she might have gone along only to please them, but in time the real pleasures of the active life would have taken over again.

Which means there would have been no trauma.

When we understand trauma in this way—*as any event that causes a change in our regular life-style*—we can spy out potential harmful traumas and defuse them. Or we can devise happy traumas—as we'll see in a moment.

First, a case of foreseeing a possible trauma. A couple learned that their five-year-old son had a visual defect. It was correctable, but only by his wearing thick prism glasses for a year. Bobby was outgoing, energetic, playful, a great favorite at his nursery school. But his parents foresaw that if he simply showed up one day at school with his new glasses, looking to the other kids like a foreign agent or a cartoon character, he would be in peril. The kids would probably poke fun at him—which would be painful in itself—but even more dangerous was the possible effect on his personality: He could withdraw into silence and sullenness, or he might adopt a mode of playing the clown-freak. In any case, at the end of a year he would not be the same boy. And his new mode of conduct might be permanent.

But his parents had an idea. They went to the teacher and told her what to expect, and together they devised a plan. Next day, the teacher, knowing what the answer would be, asked her class how many of them liked Bobby. They all raised their hands. Then she explained that soon he would need to wear special glasses so that when he grew up he'd be able to see as well as they could. The teacher talked about this necessity every day for the next three days so the children would remember it and think about it. When Bobby finally came to school wearing his preposterous-looking glasses, a few children made snide remarks, but the rest came to his aid. During the following weeks care was taken to see that Bobby continued to take part in all the school activities. He soon made peace with his necessity—and he remained the same boy. A sensitive couple and a talented teacher had prevented a trauma.

What would be a beneficial trauma? We see them all the time. Donald was fifteen and spending time with a crowd of cynical and selfish friends. He was coming to feel that kindness was a form of foolishness. He loved his parents but resented his dependence on them. For their part, they'd become afraid to ask much in the way of household chores from Donald, because they thought it would alienate him even more. Then one day the mother had a stroke. All the chores—and more—fell on him. And the outcome was marvelous. Almost overnight he became a changed youth. Loaded with new responsibilities, he carried them out, and with each act his new role came to seem more worthwhile. Notice these were not arbitrary and synthetic responsibilities imposed on him by able-bodied parents with the announced purpose of instilling discipline—which might well have instilled only resentment and desperation since the motivation for carrying them would have been fear of reprisal. These were real responsibilities—Donald was the only one who could do them. And the motivation was a desire that his mother not go uncared-for, and that the house his mother loved not go to wrack and ruin before her eyes, and also that his father not go unfed and wear shabby clothing. Now, there are cases where this would not have worked out. Donald was fortunate in that he loved his mother. If he had been coerced by his father into nursing a mother he loathed, the result would have been different. But, as it was, a beneficial trauma had befallen him.

I know of a similar case where the school bully was given the job of traffic and school-yard monitor responsible for the safety of the same children he used to terrorize. As he bent himself to the job of caring for the kids —and suppressing other bullies—his whole personality changed for the good.

This is a typical source of happy trauma: being given new responsibility. And it can happen at any age. Tim was thirty-five, intelligent but anxious and truculent, suffering from an ulcer. His chosen career was acting, and it was at a dead end. He had come to realize that he had no genuine talent. To earn his livelihood he had taken jobs in hospitals, working in the business office. Because he was intelligent, he could do his work well even though he gave it little attention. Suddenly, just when his theater work had finally ground to a halt, he was offered the job of chief hospital administrator in an old run-down facility in the Bronx. From the minute he took the job, he never looked back. He saved the hospital and saved himself as well. He was under a great deal more pressure, but both his ulcer and his truculence disappeared. He became the proverbial new man. A happy trauma.

For most of us the main sources of adult-life trauma —beneficial or otherwise—are the people we fall in love with, and the people and pressures at work. "Alice is a new woman since she met Herb." Why? Not because he treats her kindly. Because he inspires in her the wish to do new things, to act warmly and honestly. We say, "Herb brings out the best in Alice." Meeting someone new and attractive might turn out to be the beginning of a happy trauma. A new person can stop you from doing things that are hurting you. And start you doing things that help, things that get you to care about elements of the world you were blind to. This kind of person invites you to build your own self-esteem.

Sometimes a loved one gives explicit advice, out of love, and it works—because of the self creation principle. Yet the person doesn't have the Principle in mind. Phil boasted a lot. He did it subtly, but it was there constantly. Somehow he would steer the conversation around to the fact that he was once a championship mile runner in school. And then he would somehow convey what a lot of money he was now making. Rachel loved him, but not for his money or his ability to run fast. She loved him because he was funny, warm, generous—and other things. She did not in any explicit way know what he was doing to himself when he boasted, but she knew it was something bad. And, anyway, it was unattractive. So she told him so, not in an accusing tone, but in a concerned, loving one. And he conceded it immediately; yes, he knew he maneuvered conversations just to talk about his running and his money. "It makes you look anxious," Rachel told him, and that hit the nail where it needed hitting. Because it was anxiety that prompted the boasting. He wanted to look important. "I am worthy!" was the implicit message. "I'm a former running champ and I make a hundred thousand dollars a year!" The belief motivating his boasts was that if they weren't aware of his achievements they would rate him low. This is the motivation behind most boasting. Joined with it is the desire for the esteem of strangers. I'm of course not recommending contempt or indifference to strangers. But constantly extending yourself to be liked by people will build anxiety, will make you terribly dependent on what strangers think of you. And it will prompt you to prize and display the wrong credentials among the many qualities you may have.

For Phil, coming to know Rachel was a beneficial trauma. Just knowing she was in the room and loving him was enough to get him to change his style, eliminate his boasting, and reduce his anxiety.

The relationships we form in adult life can result in *bad* traumas too. They can make harmful demands of us. "Cynthia brings out the worst in Jake." That happens also. But more about that later.

Another example of a trauma which many of us have seen occur (and which results in a complete change of life attitude long after the freezing of the psyche that most psychoanalysts have told us takes place before we're five years old) is what takes place at puberty and shortly after.

We all know of the young girl who is gangling, awkward, shy, withdrawn, unsure of herself, who suddenly finds that in the space of two or three years she has blossomed into a beautiful young woman. Without much effort on her part she gets the lead in the high school musical, is pursued by a top athlete, is invited to all the parties. Ultimately this can be a good or a bad trauma, depending on how she uses the experience. But either way it might be a trauma, an event that results in a departure from a basic life-style. And this trauma potential goes with any significant personal gift that manifests itself after childhood.

But the opposite development has befallen many children too. Consider Judy, the smart, vivacious little girl who has been the social leader of the class from kindergarten right up to high school. Then something happens. As adulthood approaches, Judy suddenly realizes the girlhood cuteness has gone out of her face; she is homely. What was sturdiness in the child becomes bulkiness in the woman; she has no figure.

By the time Judy gets to college all is changed. *She* is changed. Not just in appearance, but in life-style. She runs from exposure, hides. As a freshman in high school she was the lead in the annual Shakespeare play. As a freshman in college she lacks the courage to audition for the annual class skit. She becomes withdrawn, depressed, convinced she hasn't got a chance in life. Has a trauma occurred here? Yes. Not one that has taken only three hours or three days, more like three years. But a trauma: a new factor in life that causes a change in life-style. And it's not a happy trauma.

People change. Judy's trauma took place late in adolescence. For another woman it might come twenty years later when she discovers her husband is having an affair because he is no longer attracted to her. A divorce becomes traumatic, unless it leaves one's life-style unaltered. But always note that it can be traumatic for the better.

MOM AND DAD: VILLAINS—OR HEROES? 5

Now we can get back to childhood. If a trauma is any new factor in your life that prompts you to change your life-style, we're led to ask: "Where did your first life-style come from?"

For many of us, the most important coincidence in life was the parents we were born to, because it was in response to our parents that we adopted our first modes of conduct.

Nellie was a first child. She was happy enough, the center of her mother's attention and affections and, to a less intense extent, of her father's. However, her father wanted a boy. And when Nellie was five, he got his wish. When her brother was born, Nellie was stunned to see how the attention shifted to him. She expressed open resentment of him and threw tantrums. Though mother was understanding, her father reacted with cold harshness. He became even more remote from her.

Nellie shifted her tactic. She adopted the mode of a sick, frail little girl. This didn't work either. Again her mother paid attention to her, but her father seemed only to take it as further evidence that she was an unworthy cause. He would make a dutiful stand-up visit to her bedside and disappear quickly.

Nellie shifted her tactic again. She became the good

little helpmate. Voluntarily setting the table, emptying the garbage. And tending to her young brother, who was now toddling. At last she had hit on a mode that worked: her father beamed at her. Nellie had found the right role.

By trial and error she had been searching for a mode that would achieve what she was after—her father's attentive approval. Once having found it she spent the next few years proliferating it, and reinforcing the motivation behind it.

Motivations for an act always contain two elements: a goal, and a belief that this act will help achieve that goal. Nellie's goal was her father's loving attention, and each time she acted she entrenched her desire for that. Much more critical, though, was the fact that she was entrenching her belief that the only way to achieve that goal was by being the submissive helpmate, the servant, the *utility*.

And as she grew older this mode—and this conviction —stayed with her. Why shouldn't it? It worked, and she had no insight into the harm it would eventually do her.

As she became a young adult and moved away from home, the harm took a predictable form. Whenever she met a young man she liked, her first device was to search out ways that she could serve him. If the man suggested dinner, she was quick to invite him to her place, where she would cook for him. Soon she'd be sewing buttons on his shirts, typing his work papers. It gave her reassurance—at first—because she could see she was proving her value to him, her worthiness. As a utility. She was even prompted to her first sexual experiences out of a desire to please, rather than to share pleasure.

Eventually two specific problems began recurring in her life.

Whenever a man began to get serious enough to hint at marriage she would be seized with what seemed a combination of fright and despair. She could not go through with it. Why? She couldn't say why. I can't. I'm not ready. Or something.

The second problem was that the men she became involved with consistently seemed of a type. They were selfish. Users. They were most often domineering, but were occasionally weaklings who openly confessed their need for her. In the end, they all frightened and repelled her. She couldn't see how she'd ever gotten mixed up with them.

But we can see the explanation to both problems. Whenever she got close enough to contemplate marriage there erupted from her deepest being a conviction that this man did not really love her for herself, but only as a potential unpaid servant and prostitute. The only way she knew how to attract a man was by offering herself as a utility; but then when he would choose her she couldn't believe in his love for her as anything *but* a utility. Thus the fright and despair.

And why was she always attracting users? Because the user generally has a good nose for the usable. And, an important point, even if the man were not a reprehensible user in this sense, *her own mode of operation would have made him seem so to Nellie.*

Nellie remembers being at her father's bedside when he died. It was a terrible shock to her to find that all his dying attention was for her brother, none for her. When I first met her she spoke of the event as "traumatic," a terrible wound as a result of loving her father and realizing he'd never really loved her the way she wanted.

But Nellie was wrong to conclude it was traumatic. Because it didn't change her mode at all. She made no explicit comment to herself at the time about the kind of woman her father had made her. She didn't reject her servile mode thereafter because of the shock of seeing that it hadn't brought her the love she'd wanted. The next man she met soon had Nellie in his apartment painting his walls.

Nellie's case illustrates several points. It shows *how easy it is to remain effectively consistent from childhood*

27

on, even though the Principle says you are re-creating yourself every day. Once a mode is adopted it will ordinarily stay with you unless forcibly disrupted by a trauma. If we're given no reason to jettison a mode, it will sustain itself. *Sustain itself*, almost autonomously, like a habit.

What kinds of trauma might have helped Nellie? If she had met a man who had insistently stopped her from trying to become his servant, that could have done it. Hard to come by such a man, though. Nellie has offered to cook tonight—great! Of course, there are men with insight enough to start worrying when Nellie is tenaciously doing their laundry and washing their windows. And I don't mean just worrying that she is trying to "catch" them. Men who might say, "Nellie, you don't have to do this, and in fact you shouldn't do it if you're doing it because you think it's the only way to appeal to me." There are such men, but Nellie wasn't lucky enough to meet one of them.

The second kind of trauma that could help Nellie is the kind of trauma I want this book to be. In other words, the beneficial trauma that can come from understanding the Principle and how it applies to you. In Nellie's case it was the discovery that her subservience was reinforcing her worst fears about herself—and about men. For Nellie this insight came in therapy rather than from a book. But it *could* have come without her ever going to a therapist in her life.

This helps explain another point. There are many people helped by psychoanalysts. How, when such analysts don't work at showing the effects of choices?

It's not for the reasons usually summoned up. Let's say that Nellie went to a psychoanalyst who dug back to her childhood, insisting that the whole game was fixed back then. And let's say that, true to form, the analyst dwelt on her love for her father. During the analysis it could have become evident to them both that she was always bending herself to please her father, to be a lovable slave. And it might have come to their notice that she was still doing this. The "insight" from the sessions would be that her problem was *seeing all men as her father.* And that if she understood this, emotionally grasped the truth, it would set her free. With that she might start treating men differently, and in the process alter her basic attitude toward men—and toward herself.

In such a case, psychoanalysis would, after considerable time and money spent, produce an "insight" that would send Nellie away from the couch determined never to serve a man again. As she curtailed those acts she would gain confidence. Both analyst and patient might imagine that delving into the past was necessary for change, but they would be wrong. Although they wouldn't recognize what had really happened, their work would have inaugurated a change in Nellie's mode—which would amount to a beneficial trauma. They would imagine that their understanding of the past was crucial when, in fact, the crucial thing was for Nellie to change her present actions. So the analyst did help Nellie, but, without understanding the basic principle, he couldn't use it to make the therapy really efficient.

Let's review what I've said so far. I've said the human personality is not fixed, frozen, early in life or ever. On the contrary, it is being created and re-created every day. By us. By our voluntary actions. This building and sustaining of our psyches proceeds in accordance with a very reliable and verifiable law of human nature.

I call this the Self Creation Principle. The Principle asserts that every time we act we reinforce the motivating feeling, attitude, or belief behind the act.

I've said that this Principle is the single most important key to understanding and controlling our own psychic lives. It can help us to see how we became what we are and how to change. It answers some of the most vexing questions in the history of psychology, including (with the aid of the new concept of a happy trauma) the mystery of why some people change and some don't. And it is a principle that, when understood, can be used by you, with no help needed from a therapist, to mold and remold your own personality.

This much has been said, but up till now I've had to content myself with merely asserting it, illustrating it, trying to make clear what the Principle *states*. The rest of the book will be devoted to what the Principle *implies*, and how it *applies*—to you, and all the people around you.

HOW TO BE A PARANOID 6

You too can be a paranoid. Sure it takes work, and persistence, and a certain amount of imagination, but I'm convinced that with sufficient dedication anyone can make it. And the thing to remember is that once you've started, it gets easier and easier. I can't promise you that you'll be able to convince yourself you're important enough to have thousands persecute you, but I'm sure that you can generate enough worried, anxious misery to impress your friends. This chapter will be a how-to-do-it. Next chapter: how to undo it.

Let's make sure we both have in mind the same thing when we say "paranoid." We can cite three characteristics.

The first is an *unwarranted sense of danger or persecution*. In the psychotic paranoid this can take the form of believing there's a great conspiracy afoot, masterminded by an evil genius at the United Nations, and involving the local police, your fellow employees, the mailman, the meter reader, and someone at the supermarket. The psychotic paranoid believes they are in league to discredit him, poison him, push him in front of a car. He's alternately paralyzed with fear and frenzied with self-protective activity. To protect himself he's ready to do nearly anything.

Very few people who will read this book are psychotic. But many are paranoid. They share the non-psychotic form of this first characteristic in various degrees. In its mildest form it is a persistent, generalized sense of *vulnerability*. In its aggravated form, it takes on specific messages: You're about to be fired, your wife is having an affair with the hairdresser, someone is watching your apartment with dire intent, your acquaintances would despise you if they knew the truth about your (pick one) homosexuality, Jewishness, lack of a college degree, less than 140 IQ, impoverished Italian background, lackluster record as an athlete, low income, menial job.

The second characteristic is an *unwarranted sense of how much attention you are getting or deserve to get.* Strangely enough, when you're paranoid, you think you're getting too much. The person with psychotic paranoia may think that a whole government is after him. He knows too much, perhaps has a message from God or the President. His delusions of grandeur mesh closely with those of persecution. They are persecuting him because of his greatness.

In the everyday version the person is sure that others are talking about him. The boss's door is closed—it means he's discussing me. My wife claims it's noisy in here and takes the phone into the other room—she's trying to trick me. The new memo to all employees about being on time is really directed solely at me. Those people in the corner laughing—they just made a joke about me.

The third characteristic is an *unwarranted conviction about the uncanny insight others have into the paranoid's mind.* In a psychotic it can take the form of believing that a certain person is reading his mind from a distance. "He wishes me ill. I ought to kill him before he kills me. Or, at the very least, tell the cops about it. Then we'll see some locking-up done, and none too soon."

In its everyday form, this can be a feeling of *transparency*—people see through me. My boss knows I'm lying about being sick yesterday. Jones knows I just masturbated in the lavatory. Everybody on the committee realizes I'm worried about my job. In other words, people see clearly my guilt, my motives.

A corollary of this, tied in with the first two characteristics, is the sense that you are being cunningly manipulated, tricked, outwitted. I think my wife is having an affair with her hairdresser. They're on the phone now, probably planning to meet. I'll listen in on the extension. Ah! They're talking about why permanents are bad for women's hair. But of course! They knew I'd listen in! They think they can fool me.

That's the paranoid. He feels worried. In jeopardy. He senses a conspiracy. He has a certain weakness, a vulnerability. He knows it. And *they* know it. And they're out to get him.

How did he get like this? Where does paranoia come from?

If you've got it, it came from you. You gave it to yourself. And you can take it away.

Because paranoia is the self creation principle at work in an extremely pure and observable form. Remember what we all know about habits: Every time you indulge them there is an immediate release but an eventual greater grip. Consider certain tiny paranoid habits: checking and rechecking the locks. Looking back to see if someone is watching. Tearing open the envelope you just sealed to see if you signed the check. Recounting your money. Tapping your pocket again and again to see that your wallet is still there. Constantly checking to see that your trousers are zipped or there's no wet stain under your arms.

Every time you do these things you are reinstating the clutch of beliefs that motivated them. Let's talk about the locks. The motive is a sense of jeopardy. Someone will try to get in. You must protect yourself and your possessions. Let's buy that new triple lock they just advertised. You buy it. But the bad guys saw that ad too! They'll buy one and figure it out. Let's buy that trip alarm. That goes off like a siren. But what if help doesn't come? Let's buy a gun.

Then it occurs to you they can buy a gun too. Agh, life is too much. Let's buy some sleeping pills.

In every single case, without exception, *paranoia is the result of unwarranted acts of self-protection.* Note: *unwarranted.* This is not to say that thou shalt not self-protect under any circumstances. The key thing is to know when to stop.

Or when not to start. The best preventive against paranoia is an awareness of *when* and *how* you're likely to start it going. There is a pre-paranoid state—a particular kind of situation all of us find ourselves in from time to time—that is apt to motivate us to actions that will directly create paranoia.

The two components of the pre-paranoid situation are these. First, there is *something that we in some sense possess that we especially care about.* It could be a job, a marriage, a current love affair, our new automobile—or our life.

Second, we sense a special *vulnerability* that can lead to the loss of the possession, and the vulnerability stems from some defect—real or imagined—in ourselves.

Given these two components—something you want to keep or achieve, and a fear that you may lose it through some "flaw" of your own—the impulse to start on a series of self-protective acts is strong. But with each act you will reinforce each of the motivating factors: the importance of the possession, the awfulness of your flaw, the sense that you're liable to lose your possession.

You can't avoid all pre-paranoid situations. Everybody gets into them. Because we all have things we treasure. And we all feel that we have shortcomings that threaten to disqualify us from enjoying these things. A woman who's always been a great beauty starts worrying about her age, wondering if she's still lovable. Does she start to defend herself—say, by criticizing her husband excessively, so *he'll* feel defensive and won't judge her? A young athlete who goes on to become a professional football player will start to slow down one day. Does he try to compensate by finding fault with the new players on the team—and so turn the pre-paranoid situation into full-scale paranoia?

Our *natural* shortcomings need never generate paranoia if we are careful. Even more is this true of our *imagined* shortcomings.

What are they? Example: While applying for a job at an ad agency, Charlie lies about his experience. Says he wrote copy for the ad campaign on the Slammer, the useless gadget that everyone bought in response to the thrilling copy. The lie is motivated by hope and fear. He's dying to get this job—it's with a company that makes the Slammer agency look small—and he's afraid he won't get it on his own.

It works. Charlie gets the job. But just *what* works? As soon as he starts at Ace Advertising, Charlie also starts wondering how he lucked out. Sure, he had other credentials, but maybe the Slammer campaign was the only thing that got him in. That means he's in big trouble if his new boss ever finds out that he didn't do much more than *type* the Slammer copy. This is the best job he's ever had—all his friends are impressed—and he can't stand to lose it.

Charlie has gotten himself into the pre-paranoid state. His job is important to him, but his lie might be important to the boss—important enough to get him fired. He hasn't got far to go before he makes himself paranoid about being dismissed from the job in disgrace.

Here's another example of a pre-paranoid state. Roger is forty-nine, worried because he's getting close to fifty. And he's falling for a woman, Jessie, who's almost twenty years younger. Roger looks quite a bit (at least ten years, he hopes) younger than he is, and somehow he and Jessie "never get around" to revealing ages. When they start talking about an old movie, Roger claims he saw it on TV, which he did, but he also saw it in the original release thirty years ago. He buys his clothes carefully, gets his hair touched up, manages not to run into friends his own age when he's out with Jessie. All this makes him very paranoid; he already worries at times that Jessie is secretly laughing because he's so old.

Roger didn't do anything malicious. He just wanted not to lose Jessie. But he harmed himself.

Hiding anything is a good way to become a paranoid. Why? Because it gives you a weakness—and the fear of disclosure. If you invent and promote an image of, say, a master copywriter, or a sexy young man, or someone whose family came over on the *Mayflower*, you start to believe the image is important. Superior to what you really are. You start fearing you'll lose what you want if you don't live up to that image. Add the fear of discovery to your deception, and you're likely to get scared.

There are any number of facts about yourself that you might assume would disqualify you from success. I've mentioned such things as social background and schooling. It could be something as trivial as your address: you feel it's in the wrong part of town. If you *believe* these are handicaps that may deny you something you want, you're in a pre-paranoid state. If you *act* on the belief by hiding, lying, criticizing others with the same "flaw" (or even praising them anxiously), you're on your way from pre-paranoia to paranoia.

Again: *You make yourself paranoid.* It doesn't just happen. You have to take certain steps.

It wasn't solely Charlie's lie that made him paranoid, but the lie plus his next activity. He's worried about getting fired—through being caught in a lie or found incompetent. So he works harder than anyone else, comes in early, skips lunch. Flatters the boss. And every time he does one of these things he reinforces his fear that just doing a good job isn't enough. The same fear that prompted him to exaggerate his experience in the first place.

And that lie keeps worrying him. What if he's found out? What if someone tells the boss who really wrote the famous ad copy? So he alternately tries to make sure this won't happen and checks to see if it already did. One day he notices that his boss has received a letter from someone at his old office, the home of the Slammer campaign. This must be the exposé he's been fearing; his old boss must know where he is, how he got this job. Note the sense of grandeur and transparency. By trying to compensate for his fears—lying so that his credentials will look better—Charlie has pushed himself toward paranoia. A letter from his old to his new boss *has* to refer to him.

Charlie's so worried about the contents of that letter, he decides to wait until everyone goes home and get it from the boss's desk. Telling his co-workers at five o'clock, "I'm just staying to clear up a few loose ends," he wonders if they know his real purpose. Trying to memorize the exact arrangement of everything on the desk, he worries that the boss has set a trap. (If that book isn't perpendicular to this paper, I'll know that Charlie has been here snooping.) Then he reads the letter. Whew: It's an invitation to an ad executives' luncheon. That's a relief. Wait a minute, though. His old boss is going to reveal the whole business at lunch.

There's no end to it. Every time Charlie tries to protect himself, to prepare himself for the worst, he reinforces his fear of the worst happening. Just as every time Roger avoids mentioning his age, he increases his fear that Jessie will leave him as soon as he turns fifty. (When in fact Jessie knows perfectly well he's much older than she is.)

Paranoia always comes about in this way. We're afraid of something—or someone—for some reason. We act on this fear, trying to make it go away. But every act of self-protection increases the fear, strengthens the belief that precautions are necessary.

Another example. Jean's family didn't like "foreigners." Anyone who wasn't obviously all-American (you didn't have to have blond hair and blue eyes but it helped) was suspicious. Likely to be lazy but strangely cunning. . . . Better keep away from them. ·

Jean's parents avoided all foreigners (they went abroad once but stayed with an American tour group in American hotels), and so, as she grew up, did Jean. She even turned down a job offer in Paris. And every time Jean acted on this fear—going out of her way to avoid foreigners—she *increased* it.

Then, when a number of Spanish- and Italian-speaking people started moving into her neighborhood, she panicked. She tried to form tenants' associations to keep the people out; she kept her children home from school. And even though she finally moved away (and escaped the whole problem, she thought), she found it hard to avoid the fear that the people she'd tried to keep out of her old neighborhood would hunt her down.

One of the best ways to produce paranoia is to act on feelings of jealousy, to check up on other people. After all, you're just trying to get the facts.

You think your wife is having an affair with someone at the office. She has to work late tonight: That's just an excuse—she'll be over at Sullivan's place or maybe in his arms in someone's private office. It gets to be seven o'clock, and she's still not home. Well, maybe you'll drop over to the office and surprise her; the two of you will go out to dinner. You're not checking up on her, you're just being thoughtful; there's nothing to eat in the house except leftovers.

You take a cab, you're in such a hurry. Finally, at the office, you find her alone. Working. She's pleased to see you, will be happy to go to dinner, but first she has to finish what she's doing—it'll take half an hour. And as you wait, you wonder how she knew you were coming over, how she got Sullivan out of the way in time. Was she just lucky?

As I promised at the beginning of this chapter, becoming paranoid gets easier and easier. With each paranoid act you'll increase your fear. Even so simple an act as closing your office door to make a phone call—if it's motivated by fear—has the direct effect of intensifying your sense of menace. You close the door because you don't want your assistant to catch on that you're having an affair. At first you think he's the only scandalmonger around, but when you open the door one day and see Joe from the next office lurking in the hall, you realize that he's snooping too. So you start watching Joe and your assistant. If you see them together after a phone call, you'll know they're comparing notes on what they overheard. Well, maybe you'll fire your assistant. Maybe you'll make Joe look bad at the next sales conference. Each act, each plan, for self-protection makes the enemy look larger and more powerful.

But what enemy? Joe would in fact like to be your friend. So would Lisa, who works with him and asks why you've been giving him a hard time. But you can't trust either of them. They've been listening. They know too much.

You can let paranoia ruin your life. Or you can stop it. The next chapter shows you how.

HOW TO STOP BEING A PARANOID 7

How can you know whether you're paranoid? What if your husband or wife really *is* having an affair? What if your boss *is* about to fire you? Surely it doesn't count as paranoia if your fears are warranted?

No, it doesn't. If you've been playing tennis during office hours, it may not be paranoid to stop if you want to keep your job. But if you don't go near the tennis courts during the week and haven't been goofing off otherwise, working harder and harder to keep your job may be paranoid.

What about some kind of middle ground? Suppose your boss really doesn't like you—because you're younger or smarter or simply because someone else hired you in the first place? Is it paranoid to take precautions then?

Yes, because your precautions probably won't make a bit of difference. You can't do much to change your boss's state of mind, but you can do a real number on your own. You can convince yourself that losing this job would be the end of the world, that your boss will make sure that you never work in Detroit again—you can make every one of your fears unbearable. Simply by acting on them.

There are two useful exercises that can help you find out whether you're being paranoid or sensible. Both of them involve taking the same simple steps: Stop, look, listen. Stop what you're doing, see what it is, and listen to what's going on in your head as a result. To the way your acts are affecting you.

First exercise: Stop *after* you've just done something to protect yourself. (I'll be talking about ways to recognize all your self-protective acts later in the chapter.) Figure out what you were trying to accomplish. Did you start coming home on time instead of three hours late because you honestly missed spending time with your wife or because you were afraid she'd been seeing another man? Did you buy a new lock because the old one was broken or because you'd heard of a robbery two blocks away? What was your goal?

And did you achieve it? Do you feel better now—or worse? Wait a few days and ask this question again: In the longer run, did your act *work*? Did it lay your fears to rest? If the act was paranoid, the answer will be No. Each act eventually reinforces the belief that such acts are necessary. You'll be thinking up all kinds of reasons why one more defensive act would *really* do the trick. In contrast, if you were truly taking a necessary precaution, you'll feel that you've done what you can and the matter's closed.

The second exercise works the same way, except that you stop *before* you do something to protect yourself. Don't buy the new lock and see how you feel. I sometimes call this the *method of magnification*: By denying an impulse, you cause it (initially) to swell, magnify, reveal itself more nakedly. The motivation will burst through its own disguise. If you're afraid of something, not protecting yourself will bring your fears into focus.

Pay attention to everything that goes through your head as you leave the old lock on the door. Free-associate. Write your thoughts down as they occur to you. Above all, don't censor your fears; if you're afraid that unless you get a new lock your next-door neighbor will plant stolen drugs in your apartment or your mother will come looking for your birth-control pills, write that down. Your fears will be most intense when you refrain from the acts you *think* will bring relief; the point of refraining is to make your fears conscious. Once you know what you're afraid of, you can do something about it.

These exercises help you to clarify just what's bothering you. They're also a good introduction to the way to stop being paranoid altogether. Which is: *Find the actions that reinforce your fears and refrain from them.* You'll feel worse at first; you'll have all kinds of excuses for reverting to paranoid behavior, but your fears—and the paranoia—*will* subside.

Why? In Chapter 2 I laid down the Principle: *Every time you act, you add strength to the motivating idea behind what you've done.* Turned around, the Principle tells us what to do about it:

YOU CAN WEAKEN ANY MOTIVATING IDEA —ANY FEELING, ATTITUDE, OR BELIEF—BY CEASING TO ACT IN THE WAYS THAT REINFORCE IT.

Sure. But how do we know what we're doing to reinforce our feelings?

I can't follow you around every day writing down everything you do, but my experience has given me some specific ideas. I've learned certain things to watch out for. You can learn these things too. This chapter and the ones following will train you to recognize significant choices you make in your life and the ways these choices affect you.

For example: I've mentioned the pre-paranoid state —when you care very much about something and feel you're in danger of losing it. This happens partly through circumstances and partly through your own actions.

This means the situation is frequently in your power. And if you keep finding yourself wanting success desperately and worrying just as desperately about failure, the following suggestions can help.

First, try diversifying your interests. It's not degrading The Relationship or your lifetime goal to care about a few other things as well. We can see the Principle at work here. If you *act* on the premise that a lover or a job or the ethnic purity of your neighborhood is the most important thing in the world—the *only* thing that really matters—you increase your dependence on that one thing. Which gives you a dangerous weakness for paranoia.

Sylvia was very close to her friends, until she started getting close to Mike. Then she would break appointments, not return phone calls, ignore birthdays—and her friends eventually stopped calling *her*. This meant that Mike had to be all-in-all: her lover, her confidant, her only friend. No wonder she scared easily. When Mike went away on a camping trip with some friends, she made elaborate plans to check up on him. Paranoia at work. And the Principle at work. Always putting your job or a project ahead of your friendships can have the same effect.

Or perhaps you're not that involved with a job or relationship for its own sake, but as a means to an all-important end. It's status. You've just landed the vice-presidency of World Conglomerate, and you brag about it to everyone you meet. The premise behind the boasting is that you, just *you*, aren't good enough: You need special props, like this prestigious job, to make friends and influence people. Every time you act on this premise, you increase your need for the props. If you lose the job, if your boss even shows a slight sign of displeasure, you feel terribly menaced. You won't be important any more. No one will notice you.

(The method of magnification can be very helpful here. Try not boasting at just one party and see how it makes you feel. If you start feeling worthless and practically invisible, this is a sign to stop boasting at once—not to keep on in the hopes it'll make you feel better.)

Depending on a husband or wife for status can do similar damage. Every time you stress to someone that you're married to the mayor or the boss, you reinforce the premise that you'd be nothing without your spouse, which heightens your fear of losing him or her. Overspending, displaying your affluence, showing your casualness about cash—this is another common device that can generate a form of paranoia. It can jeopardize you by making you more dependent on the source of that money you're squandering. And the tactic, motivated by the idea that casualness about money is lovable, persuades you that your lovability depends at least in part on your easy affluence. But in fact you don't have as much money as the tactic suggests. You're really a fraud! People will find out!

AVOIDING PARANOIA

Sooner or later most of us find ourselves in a pre-paranoid state no matter what. We can try to be well-balanced and keep our goals in perspective, but, well, this is the job it took three years to find and the boss always has a scowl on his face. It would be nice if he gave some encouragement once in a while, but there isn't too much we can do about it. Except worry. Maybe he wishes he'd hired someone older/younger/more experienced.

What can we do besides worry? *Nothing.* And doing nothing will help ease the worrying. The way it works is simple, if paradoxical. *Defending yourself will increase your fear; taking your chances will diminish it.*

Here it is, the Principle. Every time you act on fear—trying to protect yourself—you reinforce the premise that you're in danger. And every time you act on the premise that there's nothing to fear (which sometimes means not acting at all), you increase your sense of security.

What if you're wrong? What if your fears come true?

Usually the threat isn't nearly as bad as the paranoia.

When you take chances, you may get hurt, but at least you'll find out that you're strong enough to survive a disappointment or two. And that's better than spending your whole life on guard. If you act on the premise of durability, you will reinforce it. Act on a premise of weakness or vulnerability, and your sense of that weakness will be heightened.

To help you recognize behavior that may *seem* perfectly reasonable but that actually reinforces paranoia, here are some specific things to watch out for:

1. **Don't defraud people.** For instance, don't hide some fact about yourself from a friend because you're afraid it'll ruin things. Reveal the fact, whatever it is, and take your chances. If you hide it, you'll (a) make it seem more hideous to yourself, (b) persuade yourself of the frailty of the friendship, and (c) add a new source of paranoid worry—fear of discovery. Always ask: "What's the true motivation behind what I'm doing?" You may answer: "My love for my friend." True, and that concern for his affection will be heightened. But there are other, more specific, feelings and beliefs that will also be heightened. And they are all fears.

2. **Don't ask for reassurance from people.** Don't ask your friends if they like you, your lover if you're still attractive. Here again, stop and consider your motive—uncertainty. Acting on that uncertainty can never make it go away; it can only generate new questions and new fears. Once you've asked, *any* answer that you receive will sound suspicious. If it's what you wanted to hear, you'll be afraid that it's insincere and extorted ("What else could she say?"); if you don't get the answer you want

45

("Do you love me?" Silence), you'll be sure that your worst fears are coming true.

3. **Stop making hasty accusations of people—publicly or privately.** Take your chances—that's the key phrase—on what people will do to you. The act of accusing makes you believe more and more that people are threatening you, and may actually make you a new enemy or two. Your rage and sense of urgency about any particular threat will rise and then fall; you'll come to realize that most of your accusations had no real basis.

4. **Stop correcting people's behavior.** The motive for this again is fear—fear of how people will treat you if you don't stop them. "Don't yell at me," you warn your wife, before she has a chance to decide if she's angry or not. "Don't forget to buy me a birthday present." Prove to yourself that you can function in your relationships without getting anyone to treat you differently for a while. Don't check up on people or tell them how to behave. Simply trust them. Once you stop reinforcing your fear of mistreatment by acting on it, you'll start to realize that the people in your life often mean well.

5. **If you tend to feel an immediate need for information—and act on it by constantly making phone calls or collecting evidence—stop.** Don't call your lover in the middle of the night to see what he or she really meant by that last remark. Try to live without being constantly prepared and armed for the future. You're not only making yourself paranoid by your investigations, you're probably being a pest to others.

6. Be careful of any tendency to "sell" yourself.
It tends to isolate some single quality you have and makes your sense of self-worth depend on it. I mentioned boasting. There are nonverbal boasts too. What's going on when someone intentionally flashes a huge roll of bills, or wears startlingly revealing clothes, or assiduously displays Gucci, Pucci, Tiffany, and Louis Vuitton labels, or gets the Harvard Alumni Monthly sent to the office rather than home, or constantly exhibits the latest abstruse novel—preferably in the original German edition—on the desk or coffee table? They're selling themselves or, rather, some aspect of themselves. But they're paying more than they think. With each successful sale, they create new anxiety. They have put themselves in a contest, with a possibility of defeat that never needed to be.

Beware of the things you do well, the rarities you possess. You have to manage them carefully. If you strut those talents or possessions for approval, you're liable to become dependent upon them. You'll feel they're the whole basis for your reputation and that you'd be lost without them. Every one of us at some time feels such an impulse to convey messages about ourselves. If at social gatherings you are aware of a tension within yourself that cries out for relief-by-revelation, beware. You may be about to sell yourself.

And if after such a gathering you feel a certain anxiety and depression somehow tied to something you said or did, scrutinize. There might be other reasons, but look for this one: Did you do or say things intended to impress someone? Beyond the paranoid anxiety that selling generates, there is this jeopardy: What you're selling is not really what you want people to buy.

Those were the kinds of things to stop doing. In order to reinforce a positive outlook instead of a negative one, *start*:

1. **Thinking about other people's lives.** What are their struggles, goals, strengths, and weaknesses? Talk to people important to you, from friends and relatives to anyone who tends to make you uneasy—the doorman, your accountant, a woman at the PTA—and try to learn about their lives. What are their particular struggles? What difficulties are they working to surmount? Have you shown recognition of their struggles?

   This can save you from serious distortions later on, when you might otherwise see yourself as helpless and everyone else as strong and fully established. What you're doing is reinforcing the premise that other people are human and fallible, like you, instead of calculating and dangerous.

2. **Cultivating a sense of fun.** Enjoy yourself, especially with other people. Incipient paranoia can make you feel like a hanger-on in relationships—and constant grimness can make you one. Stop talking about your worries all the time and see if it improves your relationships—which will in turn make you less likely to feel your friends are turning against you.

It's obviously easier to take these steps in the early stages of paranoia than in later ones. But even if you're really paranoid, you'll have moments when you realize your fears are unwarranted. Cling to any glimmers of optimism: Maybe things really aren't all that bad. Believe it or not, that optimism is *not* naïve and unrealistic; it's probably a lot closer to the truth than the gloomy scenario you've got worked out.

We all tend to trust our judgment more when it predicts the worst than when it says everything will be just fine. Resist this tendency. For once, decide not to trust your judgment when it turns pessimistic and paranoid—and not to act on it. That's the important thing. You don't have to *believe* that not reading your husband's mail makes sense—just don't do it. It'll start making sense to you later.

Don't worry if you still feel paranoid at first—as long as you don't *act* on this feeling. Even while you're suffering from mild delusions of persecution, you can triumph over them—if you recognize that they're delusions and don't act on them.

Try admitting your irrational fears to a friend. Something like, "I have these paranoid ideas about getting fired. The boss hasn't said anything against me, and he gave me a raise two months ago, but I'm still worried all the time." This is different from trying to convince your friend you're about to be fired. In that case you're reinforcing your paranoia by telling the world that it's reasonable. But simply admitting that you sometimes have groundless fears (who doesn't?) can start liberating you from the belief that all hell will break loose unless you take instant precautions.

Once you stop trying to control everything that happens, you'll start taking the chances that can expose you to the best—not only the worst, as you've feared—that life has to offer.

BREAKING
BAD HABITS,
or WHERE TO START
WHEN YOU DON'T KNOW
WHAT'S WRONG
8

This is a chapter about habits. But in a sense the whole book is about habits—bad and good. How to break the bad, how to make the good.

The whole book is about habits because our convictions are not created and maintained by a single act. You have to reinforce them constantly by acting. The jealous person habitually reproduces his jealousy. The confident person makes confident choices and thereby regenerates confidence. We all repeat the same kinds of acts, and the underlying premise—jealousy or confidence, whatever—is reinforced in our minds. Every feeling, attitude, or belief that stays with you is being retained, reinforced, by strands that your own choices weave. Choices you make constantly, habitually.

We've all seen examples in everyday life. Stan knows that he's afraid of criticism; he can do something about it by recognizing all the ways (habits) he's worked out to avoid it, and by breaking them. Frank realizes he's indecisive; the next step is for him to learn what habitual moves keep him that way. And so on.

That's one approach—know the condition, then look for the sustaining habits—and a good one for working on specific problems. But habits can also be used in the opposite way: Take a known habit, and use it to hunt out the condition.

Before you can understand exactly how to do this, you need to understand just what a habit is.

A habit is the quintessential example of how the basic principle of self creation works. It is an activity you keep repeating, keep *wanting* to repeat, *just because you keep reinforcing the urge for it by acting on that urge.* If you stop acting on it, the urge will go away. There are all kinds of habits—from smoking or biting your nails to having two drinks before dinner or watching TV on Saturday nights or saying "you know" all the time. But all habits have this in common: they're voluntary and, in a sense, artificial. You create them. You can live without them. Sleeping and breathing aren't habits (although the *way* you sleep and breathe may be) because they're physical needs that will not go away if you stop acting on them.

You'd be no one without your habits: in fact, some habits are just plain necessary for you to get on with living. You wouldn't want to brush your teeth differently every day; you have better things to think about. And that, many experts have pointed out, is the virtue of habits; they free your mind for other purposes. You don't have to get up each morning and wonder, what am I going to do today and how am I going to do it? You have certain routines to get you from one place to another—from bed in the morning to work. If you didn't have any such routines, or habits, you'd be overwhelmed by the number of decisions it would take to get the simplest thing done.

But habits can also have certain vices. We've already touched on a possible one: A habit is only as good as its premise. If you spend Saturday nights watching TV because you're afraid to go out after dark, you're reinforcing a harmful idea. Of course, it can always work the other way around. Watching TV can be a good habit if you're working night and day to earn the down payment on a house and you need a few hours a week of easy, free entertainment.

But it usually takes a while to figure out the motive behind a habit. Right now, most of us couldn't say why we always wear blue suits or order onion soup in restaurants. And we don't particularly care. After all, there's nothing wrong with blue suits or onion soup.

At the same time, most of us have certain habits that we don't like. That we've been meaning to break one of these days. So now's the time. Breaking a bad habit is its own reward, and then some—it'll teach you something about yourself.

Any of these six things can make a habit bad:

1. The habit doesn't accomplish anything, but it costs you time and energy. Useless habits can also lead to complications. There was a woman who used to say "follow me?" after most of her sentences. One day she asked a gas station attendant for directions and added her usual "follow me?" To her alarm the man answered, "Sure, lady, as soon as I get off from work."

   Whether or not you've had similar problems, it's good to get rid of habits that are unproductive. They encumber you.

2. The habit draws you away from experience. You always clear the table right after dinner —even if it means interrupting a conversation. Or you keep asking people what time it is. This last habit—finding out the exact time —is especially widespread; thousands of people can't enjoy an experience without knowing just when it starts. Which is a good example of the problem with this kind of habit; it keeps you preoccupied and out of touch with what's actually going on at the moment.

3. The habit is physically harmful. Smoking, overeating, drinking too much are obvious cases. And certain other habits can cause physical problems, like constantly repressing anger.

4. The habit irritates people. You clear your throat before talking. Or ask for compliments all the time. Or drum on the table. Or hum. And you're driving your friends up the wall the whole time.

5. The habit makes you look foolish. I knew a psychiatrist who bit his nails—and got all kinds of comments from patients. He'd stop for a week or two, then start biting again when the nails grew in. Some of his patients couldn't wait to inspect his nails every week.

   This doesn't mean that you have to break every habit that somebody else doesn't like. Certainly not if the habit's important to you. But the psychiatrist realized that he didn't particularly want to bite his nails, and he certainly didn't enjoy the way it affected his appearance. So he decided to break the habit.

6. You don't approve of your own habit. It violates your own standards in some way. You habitually let slip things that people have told you in confidence. No one knows, but it bothers you. Whatever the habit is, you don't like yourself for it, and so the habit's worth breaking.

THE METHOD

You can get two payoffs from breaking habits: you get rid of something you didn't want anyway, and you get new insight. But *how* do you break the habit and get that insight?

I wish I could say you could do it without any will-power, but I can't. You have to refrain—go cold turkey. You've probably tried with some habit before, and you may or may not have succeeded. But this time you *can* succeed. Through the following method:

First, *study the habit*. Don't just put down this book and resolve never to drum a table again. Keep on just as before for at least a week. You may start to hate the habit and wonder how you ever got started. But *give yourself this week to observe the habit in action.*

As you do this, figure out just what the bad habit *is*. Define it. This is easy if it's something you want to stop altogether, but a bit more complicated otherwise. Take overeating, for instance. The bad habit isn't eating—you have to do some of that no matter what. And "overeating" isn't specific enough as a definition. Be precise; define the bad habit as, say, eating bread and cake and second portions. Then you'll know what to avoid.

Next, observe *when* you engage in the habit. What seems to bring it out in you? Are you usually with certain people at the time? How do they make you feel? The more you know about a habit in advance, the better prepared you will be to break it.

Then, after this week of observation and definition, it's time to stop. As we know, the urge for the habit will increase at this early stage, which is why so many bad habits *don't* get broken. But these pointers will help you get past that stage.

1. **Try to stop completely instead of tapering off.** If you're still smoking a few cigarettes a day, those cigarettes will renew your urge to smoke. Stopping cold is the best way to break this cycle.

2. **While you're trying to break the habit, discount any judgments of yourself that come to mind.** Say the habit is talking too fast:

when you slow down, you may think you're taking too long and boring everyone silly. But your perceptions aren't trustworthy at this stage; they're tainted by your desire to start the habit all over. So *don't act on them*, and don't worry about them if you can help it.

Keep a record of the reasons that come to mind for resuming the habit. No matter how extreme or unrelated they seem, jot them down: they contain information you can use later.

And keep reminding yourself that you can always reconsider the habit—maybe it really wasn't so bad—*after* you've gotten over the withdrawal symptoms that distort your thinking.

3. **Acknowledge your urge for the habit when you feel it.** If you pretend that it isn't there, the habit can become treacherous. You'll realize too late that you've somehow just smoked two cigarettes or delivered a five-minute speech in two minutes flat.

4. **When you feel a sudden, strong urge for the habit, try to pinpoint the situation or state of mind that came up just beforehand.** Maybe you felt lonely or foolish or inadequate in some way. Write these feelings down and be alert for any that keep recurring.

5. **Don't torture yourself about lapses.** Just try to figure out what triggered it, then get started again right away.

Let's say you just broke your resolve. You've been trying to stop biting your nails—and now, at the worst time, in the middle of a job interview, you started in worse than ever. How can you *not* hate yourself and just give up?

Well, don't. If it helps, think of yourself as someone brand new, coming in to replace that nervous person who bites his nails. And remember that today's mistakes never doom you to make the same mistakes tomorrow. Be alert to see if you start to form new habits or revert to old ones. Now that you're not smoking, do you feel the urge to start biting your nails again? Or perhaps to start biting your nails for the first time in your life? You can sometimes identify a family of related habits by seeing which impulses substitute for each other.

6. **Be careful if you use rewards to help break the habit.** There is a lurking danger: There are people who diet all week long and then reward themselves with cake on the weekend. The problem is not primarily those weekend calories; it's the renewal of the desire for the old habit of eating sweets.

If you do use a reward, it should be as far removed as possible from the bad habit itself. At its best, a reward will be useful to you in some other problem area. Example: Jo Ann felt unwarranted guilt if she spent time or money on things for herself. She was also trying to give up smoking—so she promised herself that she'd give herself an afternoon in the city for every two weeks without cigarettes.

But even a positive reward system like this one isn't as good as breaking the habit with no special reward in sight. Because with no rewards you're teaching yourself that you are strong enough to break the habit on your own. So think carefully before you use rewards, and choose constructive ones if you use them at all. The real reward will be your freedom from the habit.

7. **Remember that you won't always feel the way you do now.** That it's a temporary response to the stress of breaking a habit. And that things will improve—within weeks or possibly even sooner.

This is especially true if you're now feeling awkward or phony or even incomplete. ("I'm not myself without a cigarette in my hand.") All these are totally normal reactions as you break a habit, and they *will* go away.

In the middle of all this, when the urge for the habit is strongest, use the *method of magnification*. Ask yourself this sequence of questions:

1. Why do I want to resume the habit?
2. What am I missing or losing without it?
3. How am I harming myself by giving it up?
4. What terrible truths about myself suddenly come to mind?
5. What terrible things do I expect to happen?
6. What will people say about me?
7. Who will say this?
8. How does my present state remind me of my past?
9. What fantasies or visions of people, past or present, come to mind?

Make sure you answer these questions. If possible, free-associate into a tape recorder, saying anything that comes to mind. Don't censor your responses; the more outlandish they seem, the more useful they're likely to be.

If you feel blocked, you probably *are* censoring your answers out of embarrassment. Force yourself to say the worst out loud. Exaggerate. "I know I will die of loneliness without my poker game." "I hate myself for being fat more than ever now that I'm trying to lose weight." "Everyone will laugh at me over the holidays if I don't drink."

At the end of this process, you should have a sense of accomplishment—you've rid yourself of a bad or useless habit—and new knowledge about yourself. And this knowledge can lead to dramatic results.

Take Brad, whose habit seemed innocent enough: he was always checking to see if he had his wallet. Especially, he realized as he studied the habit, when he went out with a woman he found desirable. It got to be embarrassing; they'd be sitting peacefully at dinner, and he'd be fumbling around for his wallet.

People were starting to notice, and he felt silly, so he decided to break the habit. No problem, he thought. It's not that important to me.

Well, on his next date he learned that it *was* important. He was sure that he didn't have his money. He restrained himself from pulling out his wallet to check, and this allowed him to magnify the meaning that the habit had for him: What would happen? What would be revealed about him?

"She'll think I'm incompetent. I need my money; I'm expected to pay for dinner. She'd walk out on me if she found out I wasn't a solid person."

"Solid person," to Brad, meant someone who had money. So he always carried money (at least a hundred dollars at all times), and yet he felt anything but solid. Instead, he felt fraudulent and inadequate. He expected to be found out any minute.

When he asked himself what this experience reminded him of in his past, Brad remembered an episode in junior high school. He was on a double date at a soda fountain, and the girl with the other fellow decided on an extra ice cream sundae. When the check came, Brad didn't have his half of the total. The drugstore owner yelled at both boys, and Brad felt humiliated. He never went into that store again.

Brad hadn't thought of that incident in years. He kept on asking himself, "What is being revealed about me?" and started recalling other events in his past. And remembered the part money had played in his childhood. He was an only child, and his parents were well-to-do and protective. They wouldn't let him play in sports they considered rough or dangerous, which was most of them. So Brad spent much of his time indoors, reading or playing quietly.

When he complained that the other boys didn't like him, his parents tried to make amends. They gave him *money* to take groups of kids to professional baseball games with all the trimmings—all the junk food everyone could eat before, during, and after. At the games, Brad initiated his habit, running to the men's room to take out his wallet and count his money. Later the habit became more streamlined—he didn't need to count the money, just touch the wallet—but the gesture had the very same meaning it had when he was an insecure ten-year-old.

At the time Brad was dealing with this habit, he was twenty-eight, attractive, well-liked, athletic, and seemingly self-assured. *But his old habit kept reinforcing his childhood fears and his childhood images of himself.*

Breaking the habit was the first step toward self-esteem. The next step was looking for other habits that had the same effect. Boasting, for instance. And refusing to talk about his failures. When he came to see me, Brad had recognized that he wasn't enjoying his life, that his successes were never enough for him. Now he realized that he was mildly paranoid, that he was *making himself* paranoid, and that there were things he could do to stop it.

Another example. Richard was a professor who made huge sweeping gestures when he spoke. All his students noticed, and one day he saw a group of them mimicking him. That did it; he resolved to break the habit.

The next day, as he stood before a class without moving his arms, he had the odd thought that *he was tiny and would not be noticed.* This even though he was well over six feet tall.

Richard had been the youngest, smallest child in his family. Neither his parents nor his older brothers were all that attentive to him, so he used to wave his arms to get their attention. And this habit—with its premise that he was insignificant—persisted through his teens, when he was growing rapidly, and into his adulthood.

As he broke the habit, Richard started to look for other ways in which he made himself feel small. Except for the arm-waving he was usually quiet and deferential; after all, as a boy he knew he wasn't going to win arguments at home. He was afraid to assert himself; at the same time, he was ashamed of himself for being so meek.

Like Brad, Richard couldn't have defined this as his problem when he first came to see me; he was only aware that he wasn't happy. But breaking a habit he didn't like anyway helped him understand what was really bothering him.

It's important to realize that habits tend to come in clusters. Louise, the young girl who was raped, traumatically adopted a life-mode of avoiding and condemning sex. A *life-mode*—not just a single habitual act of avoidance, but a whole cluster of them. She refused invitations to dances, but she also adopted a very conservative style of dress and self-presentation.

In the same way, Nellie's belief that she had to be a utility was due to a *collection* of activities. Most attitudes are. The feeling of being dependent on others' opinions is reinforced by a collection of every-day habits—so is confidence, for that matter. Certainly any attitude important in your life relies on more than one activity for its present existence. To change any attitude you have to modify a cluster of habitual activities.

There's an important implication. *It's easier to try*

to break, say, five related habits at once than it is to elim-inate them one by one. (It's no easy job to find and relate the pertinent habits in your life-style, but you can do it—and surprisingly quickly once your eye is trained.) If you try to eliminate just one habit in a five-habit cluster, you're at a disadvantage. The initial habit will be harder to break because the attitude related to it will be constantly replenished by the four other habits. You *can* eliminate the one habit, but it will be harder.

You can find the related habits. In practice they tend to stand out clearly on your landscape as soon as you adjust your eyes to their coloring. And, as I say, wholesale change is actually easier than piecemeal.

If, try as you might, you cannot kill the urge for a habit by refraining from both it and other habits in its cluster, then chances are you're not dealing with a habit at all but a compulsion. That's what the next chapter is about.

COMPULSION 9

A compulsion is a habit, and something more. It is a repeated, seemingly habitual activity that differs from pure habit in that the urge to do it is *not* eliminated simply by refraining from it.

Compulsion is almost like an itchy skin condition caused by something you're eating. You scratch and there's momentary relief, but if you refrain from scratching, the itch does not go away because the *scratching* is not causing the itch; something in the diet is. Think of a habit as an itch that *is* sustained by the scratching.

Consider some typical compulsive activities. Obvious ones are gambling, drinking, overeating. Less obvious perhaps (and not always compulsive) are such things as watching TV, doing crossword puzzles, constantly cleaning or tidying up or arranging objects, list-making, manic shopping-tennis-golf-bridge—it can be almost anything if it does the job.

Many healthy activities begun for other, approvable reasons, can become compulsive if they are found to do the job: jogging, studying, working, reading.

What's "the job"? The job is *blocking awareness, deadening pain.* The job of a compulsion is to provide *escape.*

Sidney plays bridge constantly for huge stakes because he senses he is a failure in life after having shown immense promise as a student. At the bridge table his concentration is superb; the fact of his life is shut out splendidly.

Marsha watches TV for untold hours each day because her marriage is no good. The TV absorbs her attention.

Mary is constantly rearranging the books, furniture, paintings, closets at home, imposing apparent control on a world whose basic chaos she fears. She is in effect jamming the airwaves against an unacceptable message: She has certain ominous physical symptoms, but will not go to a doctor.

Fay's compulsion comes and goes. At cocktail parties when there are many young people present, she finds she compulsively overeats and drinks. She wants to escape the pain of feeling she is getting older.

Whether the compulsion is obvious, like alcoholism, or subtle, like biting one's nails to avoid a moment of passivity while being criticized, what marks the activity is its function as an escape.

Think of it as an *opiate*. Compulsion is the opiate of a psyche in pain. It performs the functions of an opiate, and has a similar gripping irresistibility.

Though it relieves pain on the spot, the ultimate effect is increased damage within. Because the premise behind it is a sense of hopelessness about coping with the real problem. Act on that premise, and you'll reinforce the idea that your problem is insurmountable.

Thus the compulsion, which is designed as an escape, actually has the effect of confirming the sense of being trapped. It tells you that your resources are inadequate for dealing with the problem directly.

The compulsive activity has other disadvantages. It dulls your enjoyment of things not connected with the compulsion itself. It demands such precedence over all other activities as to deprive you of freedom.

And, to the extent that it keeps you from *confronting* the real problem, it will keep you from *solving* that problem.

You can see why cutting out the specific activity will do little to eliminate the compulsive impulse. It is true that the habit cycle is at work on this specific level: playing bridge reinforces the impulse to play bridge. But the basic motive is the need to seize some activity to kill the pain, or dull the awareness, or work off, sublimate, the energy. If by tremendous force of will Sidney stays away from the bridge table without developing the needed insight into what's been driving him there, very possibly he'll soon find some other escape: going to the track or studying Wall Street statistics relentlessly.

It was the psychoanalysts who first said that compulsive activities are merely symptoms of the underlying problems. For them it followed that trying to attack the compulsion directly was useless; you needed to solve the basic problem first, in order to drain off the need for the compulsion.

I agree that the basic problem must be solved, but I disagree with this idea that attacking the compulsion directly is useless. It has two values.

The first is that the compulsion itself is aggravating the problem. Good organizations like Alcoholics Anonymous and Gamblers Anonymous recognize the need to attack the compulsion right away. Stop now, they urge, because the compulsion is a progressive illness. Every moment you're at it worsens it.

The second value in attacking the compulsion head on is that it helps in diagnosing what the real problem is.

The compulsive feels vaguely in the wrong; this isn't to say he doesn't think others are wrong too, but in his own deepest court, the man in the dock is himself. The "truth" that he is bent on suppressing is some message of failure, of inadequacy, of moral disapproval. Sidney can't face his failure in life, Marsha her failure in marriage,

Mary her medical fears, Fay her aging. Exactly the function of the compulsion is to shield them from confronting the real problem. Ultimately their task will be to solve the problem, but first they have to face it, and the surest route to the underlying problem is through the compulsion itself.

The attack on a compulsion starts out like that on a habit. But discoveries along the way necessitate a more subtle approach this time.

1. **Make an all-out effort to stop the activity— for a short time if you can't yet stop it permanently.** When the urge for it wells up, ask the same questions you would when breaking a habit. Emphasize these questions: "Why do I want to resume?" "What seems missing in my life without the activity?" And: "What is now crowding into my consciousness without the activity?"

2. **State the underlying problem as well as you can.** Examining your thoughts when you stop the activity will help. For instance, you're resisting smoking. It comes to your mind that you feel immature, that your friends expect you to join them with a cigarette in hand. This suggests that you smoke to dull a feeling of social inadequacy. Follow up by seeing whether in fact you do tend to smoke in social situations or when nervous about them.

3. **List the *disadvantages* of the compulsion.** What does the activity cost you—in money? in reputation? in time? How does it imprison you? How does it regenerate your feeling of hopelessness?

   Start this list immediately, and add to it as you make new discoveries about yourself.

Work at sharpening your precise statement of what the problem is: the one from which you're escaping. Use knowledge from any source you can. The better you can state the problem, the surer your work can be.

4. **State the *advantages* of the compulsion.** How does it protect you from having to deal with the underlying problem? How does it dull your pain? How does it shield you in other ways from the penalties you would otherwise have to pay?

5. **Stop building an identity that relies on the compulsion.** For instance, a man who worked compulsively at his business spent virtually no time with his family. His constant excuse was that he had to provide for them. Finally a heart attack struck, and he saw the necessity of slowing down. But his dependence on making huge sums of money had become crucial to him. He constantly played big-shot with people. He would pick up checks. He would brag about his earnings and somehow always get money into the conversation. He would offer financial advice even when it was unasked for. Always he let people know that this was his special area of expertise. And it was. But by stressing it so much he'd made it seem impossible to let go. His task now was to develop other interests and new ways of presenting himself to become fully free of the need to prove himself by his earnings.

6. **Try to identify and stop any fraud or pretense connected with the compulsion.** The alcoholic pretends he can hold his liquor. If it's compulsive eating you may say you purposely decided to break your diet today. Stop pretending. Tell at least one other person

that you feel out of control, that you're worried about the compulsion.

7. **Finally, try to identify and remove the feeling of dissatisfaction with yourself that is giving value to the compulsion.** This means uncovering other activities that are giving you the problematic feeling.

Sidney—the bridge player—gripped by a sense of his failed promise, would have to look for ways in which he is still celebrating his youth. (He belongs to the Princeton Club and goes regularly, talks with old classmates, somehow once a month manages to mention in conversation his summa cum laude degree, refer to his renowned senior honors thesis and flash his Phi Beta Kappa key. He subscribes to two mathematical journals that he thumbs wistfully rather than reads. He keeps certain academic awards framed and hanging on his wall. There is no end to the way we can sustain reverence for our former times, attachments, achievements, promise.) It's not enough to quit bridge. He needs to look for ways in which he is effectively condemning his current performance. Is he hiding facts about himself, thus creating shame? Is he lying about *amounts*—suggesting his salary, his staff, his client list are bigger than they are, thus telling himself the real numbers are despicable?

Everything we currently esteem or condemn depends on our recent actions. The past only stays with us if we constantly hold it by the hand and tug it into our future. Fay's task is to uncover those actions that are generating her fear and revulsion at old age, and she must change them. (See Chapter 23, on enjoying old age, for ways that people regularly hurt and help themselves.) Marsha's task is to confront the facts of her marriage, see if actions of her own are unwarrantedly giving her the feeling that it's a failure. If indeed it is unsalvageable, then she must make some hard decisions. Until she addresses the problem straight on in this way, she will continue to exist in a numbed world halfway between compulsion and depression. Mary, who shuns the doctor despite her symptoms, will find that if she does stop her compulsive jamming of the airwaves, the message of her peril will become intolerably loud. She will discover the real problem and see it more clearly than ever.

A pitfall of life that consistently leads to compulsion is this: *placing an excessive demand on yourself.* If you set an unrealistic standard, you will inevitably force yourself to feel like a failure. The basic preventive medicine is to *define your responsibilities reasonably.* To be able to say: These are the reasonable demands that can be made of me in life. Have I met these demands? If I have, but I still feel something is wrong, chances are I am making demands beyond these, demands that are unrealistic and that are evoking a strain that can blight my life.

The chief form taken by excessive demands on oneself is an *overcommitment to the lives of others.* I'm not about to say that "Number One" is the only one that counts, or that *any* commitment to others is foolish. On the contrary, acting on that philosophy would convince you that it is a vicious, selfish world; that you are isolated; that people are there only to be used. Notice that those who talk about Number One seldom talk about children. How can they? Where's the justification of taking care of anyone who isn't Number One? If they argue that their children are their own flesh and blood, an extension of themselves, so taking care of them *is* taking care of Number One, then we ask: What about adopted children? How is it that so many foster parents have drawn such satisfaction and happiness from caring for creatures who are *not* Number One? What happens when a colleague who is also a close friend suddenly loses his "usefulness," gets ill and cannot help you but only needs help? Just think of the premises about the world that you're reinforcing when you abandon him. What a wretched vision of the universe is created by that philosophy. Not just cold and isolated, but paranoid, anxious and, should you lose whatever currently gives you the upper hand in relationships, depressive.

So I am not saying have *no* concern for the lives of others. I am saying be sure the concern has reasonable bounds. And by "reasonable" I mean not only that your burden should be humanly tolerable but also that you are not assuming burdens that are misconceived, unnecessary, not really the only possible way to contribute to the happiness of others. If Lester the insurance man, by persisting at work he hates in order to supply his family with a glossy apartment, good schools, summer camp, expensive clothes, thereby makes himself an explosive bundle of rage that his family fears and avoids, he has done the wrong thing.

Gordon, who goes furiously to work seven days a week, is in some sense of the word killing himself (perhaps even in the literal sense) for his firm. Is this reasonable? No. But people do it.

"But what else can I do?" they cry. "I'm trapped."

No, you're not. I have almost never seen a trap I believe in. There is always a tolerable way out.

Where the self creation principle helps the compulsive and the enraged is in uncovering those actions that are convincing them of the necessity of truly unnecessary commitments. This sense of a necessity to perform stems characteristically from certain types of actions. Don't display.

Don't brag. Don't apologize for lapses in those areas where you are inclined to excel. Don't take on unreasonable assignments for fear of not being liked if you say No. Allied to these are other actions: Don't hide problems, don't concede all the time. Don't demand that others match your standards.

Do these things and you will maintain frustration, a sense of being crowded, being trapped, not understood. You'll develop a fire whose heat will be released in compulsion or rage.

To fight compulsion, a dual attack is necessary. You have to refrain from the behavior, *and* you have to deal with the problem the behavior was designed to muffle.

In fact, you don't have to solve the basic problem to feel relief from the compulsion. It's enough that you've faced the basic problem, acknowledged it to yourself fully. If the problem is out in the open and you are ready to keep it there until it's solved, the compulsion does not have its former value to you. Its function was to hide the truth from you. (And its effect was to tell you that remedy was hopeless.) If you're facing the truth, the compulsion is demoted to habit, and refraining will kill it.

Stopping the compulsive activity helps you understand the basic problem, and dealing with the problem makes it easier to stop the activity. Millions of people in different self-help groups have rid themselves of compulsions. The self creation principle provides a rationale for what these groups have discovered and accomplished.

DEPRESSION, 10
orTHE HARMFUL ART OF DOING NOTHING

Depression: the feeling that life is hopeless, nothing matters, existence is misery and there is no remedy.

In its milder, most common form, it's a condition millions of us endure for long periods without realizing it. We may do things, but, oh, the energy it demands. We enjoy ourselves on brief occasions, but not nearly enough. Intensity is gone. The simplest chores seem monumental —and pointless. Unanswered letters pile up. Things that once brought pleasure seem empty: sex, friendship, achievement, a day in the country. Other people who look bright and happy seem remote. They also seem naïve— and even dishonest.

We can feel ourselves slow down. We speak, think, react slowly and dully. No effort seems worth the candle. The truth is, we're ready to quit.

No. The truth is we *have* quit. Because the essence of depression is *non*-action. Refraining. Because effort is futile. And every time we refrain, we reinstate the premise of futility.

The only kind of act the depressed person embraces is *withdrawal*.

Except in those cases traceable to a problem in the

body's biochemistry, permanent depression always depends on daily decisions.

The key to the treatment of depression is the same as that for a habit. Because depression *is* a habit. You beat a habit by refraining; you beat depression by refraining from refraining. *Do* something! Act!

To the depressive's question "Why bother?" the answer is that every time you do bother you give points to the idea that change is possible, that there are goals worth pursuing, that something *is* worth the candle. Every time you give up on something it causes pessimism and gloom (especially if you don't start something else of importance to you). If you decide you're too far behind in a contest and cut down on your effort, you'll quickly fall into a lackluster drift that is a form of depression. Quit on yourself, stop investing in your potential, and you create hopelessness.

Don't decide in advance that depression can't be changed. Because in fact it works, I've seen it; depressives can cure themselves. Depression is a habit, and people do break habits—by refraining, when exactly their initial lament was that they found it impossible to refrain.

First, let's glimpse three kinds of depression.

One kind I call *flash depression*. Things seem fine, but then quick as a flash something happens. You make a stupid comment to a client and offend him. You feel like an idiot. You plunge into despair; you imagine you've altered things forever, can never be forgiven.

Or you've had trouble with a friend, and imagine that the person no longer cares for you. The fact that you've had worse trouble in the past is no consolation. You plunge into despair first over one thing, then over another.

Another common form is often called *reactive depression*: an apparent prolonged reaction to some truly bad blow in life. You feel as if life was so good before the calamity and can't even be adequate from now on.

Wordsworth caught the experience of reactive depression in the following verse:

There was a time when meadow, grove, and stream,
The earth, and every common sight,
To me did seem
Apparelled in celestial light, ,
The glory and the freshness of a dream.
It is not now as it hath been of yore;—
Turn wheresoe'er I may,
By night or day,
The things which I have seen I now can see no more.

Instead of *reactive depression*, it's useful to call this condition *traumatic depression*, because it follows from an event that has prompted a change in our regular life-style.

The third form I want to mention is *cyclical depression*. It seems to come and go at intervals. Sometimes you can identify a regular connection—it comes at Christmas or New Year's, on a birthday; or, for some women, it ties in with their period. For others, it's as seasonal as April and November. For still others, it seems unpredictable altogether, not tied to any event or date.

Each of these calls for its own special set of tactics in combating it. I'd like to review some of these, and then give a general list of tactics that will help against all self-created depression.

For example, the first thing the person undergoing flash depression should do is ask himself how long he has had the critical information that's making him despondent. Very likely, not long: "Two hours." Couple this fact with the awareness of your vulnerability to flash depression, your readiness in the past to exaggerate how much is lost, and you'll be in a better position.

Better position to do what? To resist the impulse toward depression-inducing acts. All enduring nonbiochemical depression stems from ongoing actions.

A second tactical defense against flash depression is to

list the last five such bouts you've had, and see what they have in common. Something you did or said? Or someone else did? How permanently disastrous was the event? (Remember to conjure up *all* such events, not just some single event that *did* end a relationship permanently.) This awareness of your tendency to react catastrophically will be directly helpful in defusing such events in the future.

Also take note of depressed people around you and of how you behave with them. You may suffer from over-suggestibility, especially if you like people and naturally know how they feel. You must beware of over-identifying with them.

Speak up and tell such people that they see the gloomy side of things; or, at least, keep this consciously in your own mind about them. Keep identifying their sorrowful conclusions so that you see the other side of things. If it's a loved one, you have a double stake in not going along with despondency. You want them to pull out of it for their well-being as well as your own. You may even ask the person not to tell the same tired old stories, or use the same jokes. If he does anyhow, you may be annoyed, but you're less likely to become depressed.

The key tactic in fighting *traumatic* depression lies in not abandoning the whole style of life you had before the event. After Hugh's wife died, he dropped whole clusters of activities he used to enjoy, friends he used to see, places he used to go. He avoided familiar restaurants, skipped social functions (without even answering the invitations). He dressed indifferently, talked in a low voice, as if he didn't care whether people heard him, as if his own words weren't important any more. The motivating conviction behind all this was that nothing really mattered any more—not these people, not even himself. Acting on that motive reproduces despair. Hugh had quit.

The person in the depths of traumatic depression must ask himself: "Am I acting out of any allegiance to the past?" You may find when you force yourself to do new or pleasant things that they seem unfair, almost disloyal. Hugh discovered he had a strong inclination not to enjoy life in any way now that his wife was dead. He flinched at the contrast between her lying entombed and his playing golf.

When you can see an allegiance like this prevailing you have to question its rationality. Would the other person have wanted it? Especially if she knew its self creation effect on you? You do not honor the dead by burying the living. If you can identify a vague motive of guilt, realize two things: Acting on that motive does no one any good (you cannot restitute the dead), and forever acting on that motive will leave you forever feeling guilty.

There are other sources of traumatic depression. For example, ask yourself: "Have I made any major compromises with my basic ethical beliefs?" For instance, you've been depressed ever since you started selling some product. You realize that you think the product is harmful but haven't allowed yourself to know this. Your depression may last as long as you're fleeing from this unresolved conflict. You may have to sell something else.

Probably it was by compromises that Wordsworth dulled his spirit and drained away his genius. When young he was an idealist. But then, within a short time, he made some meaningful decisions. This great lover of nature abandoned his own child in France when the revolution broke out; he compromised his politics, and left many poets once inspired by him feeling betrayed. It was after that period of betrayal that he lamented his decline of poetic vision, and though he continued to write for half a century, it is widely agreed that he never approached the joy or boldness of his early work.

The first line of defense against *cyclical* depression is an early warning system. Know which dates bother you; if it helps, mark them on your calendar. Even if there is a biochemical element, knowing ahead of time when depression is likely to arrive helps you to avoid swelling it through the wrong kind of action, or through total inaction.

A man I know discovered that, about a day before depression hit him, he tended to lose track of time and sit in a chair for long periods without doing much. He used these cues as a warning not to withdraw from people, cancel appointments, or give up stating opinions. He would force himself to take a guitar lesson the next day. By recognizing his early warning signals, he was able almost immediately to reduce the impact of the depression considerably.

When you get depressed, start listing the things—even small things—you do only when you're depressed. Maybe you stop saying hello to people in the elevator. Or turn down invitations to parties. Or read more detective stories in two weeks than you normally read in six months. Or stay home from work. Or don't get dressed all day. These are small acts, but not harmless ones; they're all ways of withdrawing instead of fighting back. Which is what this kind of depression is all about.

With cyclical depression tied to specific occasions—holidays and birthdays, for example—it's essential to try to make explicit what message the occasion has for you. Passover reminds you of all the huge, convivial seders of years gone by. You're alone now. An upcoming Passover looms like the symbolic empty chair, except that it will be forever empty. Very often people seize exactly the wrong tack for dealing with this: they refuse all invitations for special holidays. They choose to be alone, and thus elect loneliness. With cyclical depression it's important to recognize all the early warning cues and dates, but then *always focus on what you do thereafter.* That's where the key to relief lies.

Now for the general rules to combat any kind of depression. For those who want to know how to resist the onset of the next low, or to root it out if it's on them already, here are sixteen ways of warding off depression, of forestalling hopelessness, of acting in such a way as to maintain a belief in the potential of life:

1. **Impose order in your life where you can.** Try to be on time for appointments, to answer your mail and balance your checkbook, to have food in the kitchen, to eat regular meals, to be in bed at a reasonable hour whether or not you think you can sleep. Order simplifies your life, letting you get more done with the energy you have. And everything you do accomplish reinforces your sense of worth and competence.

2. **Look after your appearance.** Keeping yourself clean, dressing presentably, even keeping your room neat, may have been difficult all your life. And maybe it didn't much matter at one point; it was a sign of individuality or rebellion or concern with more important things. But it's hurting you now—by reinforcing the idea that there's no reason to be at your best, or that you can't manage your own affairs. If you can possibly afford it, buy some clothes you like and wear them. The effort to look good will help you feel there's something to look good *for.*

3. **Don't let yourself give up a project while you're depressed.** Right now your perceptions are gloomy; it seems easier to drop out of school or to quit trying to write your novel. But force yourself to keep at it.

4. **Don't suppress strong emotions, especially anger.** You spend hours shopping and cooking dinner for your friend, who cancels at the last minute; tell her that you're annoyed. Don't say, "Oh, it was no trouble." It *was* trouble. Resigning yourself to mistreatment

makes you believe you *deserve* mistreatment —and that you'll always get it.

Don't try to suppress strong emotions in others, either. Two friends start yelling at each other; don't try to calm things down. Or, if it makes you uncomfortable to hear someone railing against a friend or the super of your building, rush in to defend the accused party. Instead of trying to get others to be as calm—and depressed—as you are, you need to learn to feel strongly and act on your feelings.

5. **Study and learn something new each day.** Learning gives you the sense that the future has new things to offer, that the best of your life isn't over.

6. **Meet all challenges you possibly can.** And decide for yourself—honestly—what you can and can't do. Perhaps your family is willing to make allowances for you ("I guess Mae doesn't feel up to having dinner with the rest of us") but you know you can do it if you try. Even if others will excuse you, don't excuse yourself from challenges you *can* meet, or meet with effort.

7. **Stop talking about your problems for a specified period.** Try it first for a day, then a week. If you stop complaining, you may make important discoveries about yourself. And talking about problems is often the single most important way a depressed person keeps the depression going; since he talks about nothing else, he comes to feel that his life must *have* nothing else to offer.

8. **Act ethically toward others, even about small things.** As people get very depressed, they tend to imagine that how they treat

other people doesn't matter. They neglect to thank people for great favors and may come to expect special treatment. All of which isolates them from the normal give-and-take of human contact, and makes the depression worse.

9. **Differentiate among people as much as possible.** Depressed people often start treating everyone the same way, which can lead to the feeling that nothing or no one is particularly worthwhile. Notice when certain friends have faithfully telephoned you, and be sure to give them good news when it comes. Or go out of your way to give pleasure to someone you really like. If you reward your own friends, you're more likely to believe that friendship can be rewarding.

10. **If you've ever liked animals, get a pet and take good care of it.** Caring for a dog or cat has given millions of people something definite to live for.

11. **Don't compare your life with other people's.** What matters is how you feel, not whether someone else might have more advantages. Starting to make comparisons usually signals that depression is on the way.

    While it can be depressing to think everyone else is better off than you are, it's also harmful to look around and say that other people have it *worse* than you do, with worse jobs, worse debts, worse marriages. When you do this, you're often talking yourself out of trying to change ("I guess I'm not so badly off next to Joe"), and changing is the only way you can conquer depression.

12. **Find as many ambitions for yourself as you can.** If you even get flickers of desire to do

something—to get a part-time job or join a choir or take a trip to Argentina—mention these desires to someone. And start thinking about them and working toward them. Commit yourself to wanting something.

13. **Take note of good moments in your life, especially the ones that come at unexpected times.** You just met an old friend by chance and spent a wonderful ten minutes with him. Why did you enjoy seeing him? Can you see him again? Arrange your life to give maximum exposure to every pleasure you can think of.

14. **Do something you've never done before.** Force yourself to talk to people you've never spoken to before.

15. **Try to spend time with people who are energetic and hopeful.** Don't make the usual mistake in depression of hiding in the company of others who feel as you do. If you can, put yourself among people energetically pursuing life.

It won't be easy at first. If you're depressed you may find such people irksome, even noisy. They are busily giving opinions, talking about the future, seeing the good in people as well as the bad. They make a demand for originality by the very variety of their interests. Conversations with them are more challenging. No matter that their very energy may seem a rebuke to you. Spend time with them anyhow, if they'll have you. You'll see your own harmful choices, and their premises, more sharply by contrast than alone. Besides, these people will not be threatened by your progress the way depressed people might.

16. **Snatch at all fleeting moments of intensity as if they were life rafts going by.** Avoid what is repetitive and automatic as much as you can. Look for experiences and activities to which you can bring a feeling of freshness and emotionality. Stop telling the same jokes or stories over and over again. Gamble instead on having nothing to say and feeling anxious. At least you can grow something valuable out of this kind of soil. The other is worthless.

Okay, but suppose there's a real tragedy, what then? It may take the form of losing your job or being retired against your will. The precepts above still apply. The point is to make sure that you do not abandon all effort, ambition, pursuit. If you're not at retirement age, keep looking for a new job. Don't, out of embarrassment, avoid old friends and locales. Don't withdraw. Don't hide. If it's absolutely impossible to find work in your chosen field or location, then move on (but it's important to make sure it's absolutely impossible; if any part of you knows you're quitting prematurely, the rest of you will get that contaminating message in a hurry). The important thing is to keep acting on the premise of hope.

Let's even address the seemingly ultimate justification for depression: The doctor has told you that you're dying. There's no denying the hideous first impact of such news. But consider this unblinkable fact: Many people who know they are dying are not depressed. They may have been temporarily, when they learned their fate, but it did not stay with them. How come?

In every case that you examine you will find the key is their program of action. Either they persist in doing exactly what they've always done or, if they change, it's to try certain exciting projects they've always dreamed about. If you allow the news to be traumatic, in the sense of altering your life-style, you may indeed be depressed for the rest of your days.

Hope never abandons you; you abandon it.

This implies that we should pause momentarily before urging an afflicted person to "take things easy." As long as he's still doing *something*, okay; but if we talk him into giving up all effort, it may be a disservice.

In the novel *The Broken Year*, by Richard Brickner, about a young man confined to a wheelchair by an accident, the protagonist asks his attendant, "Do you think I have a future?" and the attendant answers, "As a pole-vaulter, no; as a man, yes."

The story reminded me of a patient I once had. Lyle was a gifted athlete who had an accident on a trampoline and was confined to a wheelchair. Lyle's case exemplified an essential truth for all of us: We must define our "job" in life—in the broadest sense of "job"—realistically. In the end we can ask ourselves, have we done *this* job, not some other unreasonable assignment we may impose on ourselves. In Lyle's case the reasonable goals of life changed abruptly one day in a gymnasium. If he were to spend the rest of his days doing nothing because he could no longer hope to be in the Olympics, he was doomed to depression. My assignment with Lyle was to help him to see a new but nevertheless cherishable job for himself.

I knew that any choices, no matter how small, that had as their premise a certain belief in an ability of his, would strengthen his belief in that ability, and thus his belief that life still had possibilities for him. Lyle's parents had remarked to me that he'd been interested in mathematics at school, though he'd not turned his mind to math or anything else since his accident. I used to have conversations with Lyle, and his characteristic posture was slumped in his chair with his head lowered, staring at his lap or the floor in front of him. One day I mentioned a certain problem in mathematical probability that I'd recently heard. It was a simple problem in that the question was understandable immediately, but the solution was tricky. I monologued about the problem for a while, skirting any progress on it. Eventually Lyle made a soft comment, seemingly addressed to his left shoe, about an aspect of the question. Exchanges followed. They became faster and more audible. At last, along with the comments I was hearing, I saw something wonderful: his eyes. Lyle's chin had come off his chest, and he was looking at me and speaking, for the first time since I'd met him, with some force. His eyes were alert, engaged. Whatever the accident had done to his legs, it hadn't hurt his brain and that was obvious to both of us.

Two days later his mother called me, exhilarated, to say Lyle had done what she called the "first positive thing" she'd seen in eight months: he'd picked up a book. What book? I asked. An old college textbook, she said. On statistics. And he was reading it. And he was asking for pencil and paper. And he was scribbling. Lyle, I said to myself, you're on your way.

HOW TO DEAL WITH INFURIATING PEOPLE **11**

Perhaps you don't have the general problem of getting angry. It's not as if you're full of rage. But still there are one or two people—your old friend, your neighbor, your father-in-law—who put you in a rage time and time again.

Like Carol, who always seems to be insulting you. Anything you do, she can do better, or she knows someone who can. When you're with her, you start to show off, to defend your accomplishments, perhaps to exaggerate your prospects. You try to disparage her in return. And all the while you're getting more and more angry and disgusted; you not only can't stand Carol—you don't like yourself much either.

The people who make you angriest may well be the ones you love most; a full-fledged enemy can rarely drive you as wild as someone close to you can. And certainly not as often.

There's a reason for this. We know who our enemies are and why, but we often deny we have troubles with people we care about. So we make excuses for the people who make us angry, or deny that the anger is a real problem—until the next time, when we feel the rage starting up again.

Who makes you angry in what way? You may or may not know the answer at this moment. But start keeping track of your anger: who's involved, what he does, how you feel, what the issues are. If you're always angry at the same person, you'll probably find he's doing something specific that rubs you the wrong way.

For example, here are nine patterns of infuriating behavior that often go unrecognized.

1. Victim stories. John doesn't make you angry at him—just angry on his behalf. He's always telling you the ways other people mistreat him, take advantage of him. His boss misinterpreted something he said. A cab driver was abusive. A relative lied to him. John comes to you all the time with these stories, and every time you get angry at the other people. But of course there's nothing that you can do.

2. Hearsay reports against you. He tells you that a friend or neighbor disapproves of you, then makes you promise to keep things quiet. "Don't you dare tell him what I said to you." You can't confront your accusers; all you can do is listen to the report and seethe inside. Again a sense of impotence adds to your rage.

3. Promises that never come true. "Next week I'm going to start looking for a better apartment for us." "I'll stop drinking after this weekend." "A year from now we'll be rich."

4. Insistence that you feel a certain way. John expects you to get angry or nostalgic in response to a story. Or he tells jokes, laughs uproariously, and waits for you to do the same.

5. Constant questions or small requests. No matter how many favors you do, or how many questions you patiently answer, John will always be able to come up with just one more. And sooner or later you lose your temper.

6. Repeated suggestions that you're doing something wrong. For instance, John keeps a lookout for contradictions in what you say. "But last week you said you were glad to see the Smiths." "If you don't like L.A., why did you go there on vacation three years ago?" Or John can make you feel stupid in countless ways: "Didn't you realize that it was likely to snow?" "Didn't you notice that he was married?" "I can't understand why you're doing it this way."

7. Frequent reminders of everything he's done for you.

8. Denial that anyone ever has hostile motives or acts unfairly. You've just left some obnoxious people at a party, but when you mention that you couldn't stand them, John looks at you with surprise. "You're just oversensitive," he says.

9. Refusal to pay attention to anything you have to say. John can tell you his problems for hours, but when you start talking about your own, he says, "Well, I can't waste any more time now; I've got to get back to work."

The most important first step in dealing with an infuriating person in your life is to start being true to the way you feel. State your opinions. If, for instance, the person tries to tell you how to react, remember that you have as much right to your responses as he does to his. "I just don't find that joke as funny as you do." Or, "You may think they're wonderful people, but I can't stand their racist remarks. I don't agree that they never mean any harm."

You might also want to ask the person to discontinue the activity for a while. "Please don't ask me any more questions for a time, not even minor ones." Or, "Could you not make any promises for the next month?" Don't apologize for the request. But if it's not heeded at once, make sure the person understands how uncomfortable his actions have been making you. It's beside the point whether the same actions would make *him* uncomfortable. The answer that you're "oversensitive" or that he doesn't understand your reaction can never provide justification for causing you pain. The person says he wouldn't care if you kept pointing out his mistakes and never complimented him. Maybe. But this has nothing to do with the way you feel.

When you ask the person to stop, take care that you don't attribute harmful motives to him. His motives are unimportant. You merely want him to stop so that you can get rid of your feelings of anger. It's enough that you have these feelings and are asking a friend to honor them.

The worst may happen. The person can selfishly refuse to stop, which is much the same as saying he doesn't care how you feel. But it's better to learn this and have it over with than to spend years in frustrated rage because you're afraid that you'll find it out.

Or the person may find himself unable to stop. He apologizes for his habit, he can see that it might be irritating, but then he keeps on reminding you of all the things he's done for you. Or he goes on making promises so that you won't dwell on the ways he's let you down so far. Perhaps his behavior is compulsive. But you have a right to remind him each time. And admitting what the problem is—and recognizing it when it comes up—may help to diminish your rage even if your friend can't stop his irritating behavior.

When and if the infuriating situation comes up again, don't do anything designed to prove yourself or justify your behavior. If your friend ignores something you have to say, don't get in a shouting match with him. Call him aside and ask him to let you speak. Or if someone starts telling you all your faults, don't respond by pointing out all your virtues. The more you allow an attack to influence your behavior, the more important that attack becomes to you.

Let's consider an example. Ursula, who was often short-tempered with her husband Tom, realized that Tom didn't listen to her. They'd spend a whole evening talking —about him, his work, his fears, his plans. Ursula would try to get his attention but then give it up in disgust and fury.

Ursula never actually expressed her feelings about this to herself or anyone. She never said, "I don't think Tom really cares about me." Instead she went out of her way *not* to test him. When the doctor told her after her check-up that there might be something wrong, she didn't let Tom know. Her excuse was that she didn't want to worry him, but actually she was afraid that he wouldn't care. So if he didn't know what was going on, she couldn't be hurt by his indifference. Ursula went through the same routine whenever anything important to her came up—a tense situation at work, some worry about her family. She simply didn't tell Tom. And the result was a lot of anger.

Ursula came to see me, and we established that this was the way Tom was making her angry. But then what? "Act," I suggested, "as if he were not guilty. Tell him everything you'd expect to be able to tell your husband, that you'd expect your husband to care about. It's better to know where you stand than to keep on assuming he's not interested in you."

At this point there were two possible outcomes. Ursula could find that she'd been wrong about Tom, that he'd kept talking about himself out of nervousness and because she'd been so self-effacing.

Or, Ursula could find she was right, that Tom would sidetrack the conversation no matter what she had to say. That he would mutter, "That's interesting," or, "I'm sure it will be all right," before changing the subject back to himself.

When Ursula finally mentioned a problem at work that was troubling her, Tom did find a quick way out of it. He complimented her. "You're strong. You can handle it." But I'd recommended that Ursula tell Tom how she really felt, instead of letting him change the subject and hating him for it. So, after he'd started to resume his speech about the best place for their vacation, she managed to say, "Why don't you listen to me? I'm really worried."

We might say that relationships, like individuals, have personalities. And that the personalities are formed in much the same way in both instances. It starts with a feeling, then with actions that reinforce the feeling and keep on reinforcing it if the actions are not changed.

The first time Ursula said, "Why don't you listen to me?" Tom was surprised—he didn't realize he hadn't been listening. And he *did* think Ursula could handle the problem at work. But that, she pointed out, didn't keep him from telling her about all his problems. They were up half the night arguing about it. But, at least, Ursula felt Tom was listening. And the argument, which broke a long-standing pattern in their relationship, did the marriage and Ursula immense good.

In all the infuriating situations, you may sense the real problem runs deeper. The person must be avoiding you or finding fault with you because he's upset about something else. Ask him what's wrong. If there's any hope for the relationship, he is obliged to tell you what you've done. Then you can apologize if you feel you've been wrong (and remember that the other person is as entitled as you are to dislike certain things irrationally), but be careful not to confess to any motives that you don't feel. The other person may be oversuspicious. Tom, for instance, told Ursula that he started talking so much about himself because he thought she looked down on him. "You think I'm not as good as your father because I don't make as much money." And Ursula, who had never thought anything of the kind, answered, "I'm sorry you got that impression," which was exactly right; she expressed concern but didn't take on needless guilt. In any case, you have the full right not to go on being punished in subtle, infuriating ways for anything that you've done.

Perhaps the worst is true. It is a lover who is out of love. Finding this out is the risk you take when you bring your annoyance out into the open. But there's not much point in going on with someone who doesn't want the relationship enough to stop tormenting you. No relationship is worth the agony of being in continual fury at the other person. And no relationship can reach its potential until you find the cause of the fury and eliminate it.

Sometimes the person is leading you not into open fury but into a dim anxiety. Here are a few ways in which he or she may be doing it.

1. He's not treating you seriously. You haven't wanted to acknowledge any problem to yourself because he's an old friend, and you've had many good times together. But he has always treated lightly things that are important to you. He may even have come out and said that you "take yourself too seriously" or are "too sensitive." Your muffled anxiety arises from the sense that you're being abused and is compounded by your persistent silence about it. Each choice to defer to his rejection of your feelings has the effect of seconding his motion: You're rejecting yourself. Don't do it. Speak up. What *feels* important to you *is* important to you. You've got to make this choice: Either you change clusters of actions to make your areas of serious concern coincide with your friend's; or you say, No, I have a right to be different from him, and he has a duty to respect that difference. What you can-

not do (without anxiety, and, possibly, fury) is on the one hand to maintain certain standards through certain actions, and on the other to disparage those very standards by actions such as fearfully remaining silent when they are attacked.

2. He's disparaging you obliquely. Not open insult. *That* you'd spot and could cite without having it denied. It's when the disparagement is just oblique enough to invite you to get the message but not have to acknowledge it (the raised eyebrow, some light sarcasm, a snicker). But you *do* have to acknowledge it. Don't endure it silently. And make sure your response is in terms that can't be dismissed; e.g., don't say to the raised eyebrow, "I can see you don't believe me." Say, "The way you raise your eyebrow makes me feel you don't believe me." He can always deny his intention, but he cannot deny the objective fact of an eyebrow moving, or of your feeling.

3. He's always challenging you to perform. Before you even enter the room where Jason is you can feel the tension building up. You know the salon volleying is about to begin. The solution is simple: don't play. Realize you're going to feel vapid, even stupid, at first, but eventually you'll feel worlds better. Consider: Jason doesn't manage to entice Bob into his contests, but Bob doesn't look stupid. And he looks a lot less anxious than you and Jason do. Every time you let Jason pull you into one of his verbal racquet games, you are reinforcing a basket of bad motivations.

4. He is asserting his supremacy—again obliquely. You're not rich, he is; presto, the

conversation drifts again and again to his possessions. You're not married, she is; let's focus on the irreplaceable joys of wedded life. She went to college, you did not; let's sympathetically discuss the silly prejudice against non-graduates. Notice that no open put-down is involved, just a constant turning of attention to your tender spots. If you let it continue, and join in, you're doing yourself a disfavor.

5. She has a hidden agenda for you. Your mother has just introduced you to someone, and you know she now wants you to talk about your scholarship or your luxurious new home: Your assignment is to awe these people. Another example of hidden agenda: The vice-president tells you terrible things about the office manager and then asks for your conclusions. He's hoping to get a quotable denunciation from you. You'd feel anxiety if you sensed the pressure but didn't know what was expected of you. And if you *could* see what he's angling for, as you can with your mother, the anxiety stems from a feeling that you are letting the other person down. These are classical dilemmas in that either choice leaves you with distress. The rule of the Principle here is this: You will ultimately feel worse if you let concern for someone else's good will pressure you into doing something you consider basically wrong or ugly. Lovelace's lines,

> I could not love thee, Dear, so much,
> Lov'd I not honour more,

have this element of truth in them: If you

sacrifice self-esteem, you suffer a diminished
ability to enjoy what you've gotten.

The lesson throughout this chapter has been the
same: It's not what others are doing to you that counts
in the end. All they can do is tempt and threaten, expose
you to a message. It's what *you* do that will determine the
final impact that other people have on you. It should go
without saying that this doesn't mean someone can't have
an impact on you by shooting you with a gun or injecting
you with drugs. Nor does it mean that evidence alone
cannot change nonpersonal "beliefs" of yours such as the
date of Napoleon's death or the melting temperature of
tin. (But even there your readiness to *accept* the evidence
stems from actions that have persuaded you the source of
the information is worthy.) It does mean that no coercion
can directly change your personal feelings and convictions *permanently.*

Such feelings as fury, fright, joy, and dismay can
sometimes be caused in you directly by someone else's
action. But the key point is that if they are not *sustained*
by your subsequent actions, they will start to fade immediately from the mind's screen. Even the effects of "negative reinforcement therapy" inflicted on homosexual men
(whereby through drugs they are induced to vomit at the
sight of a photo of a nude man) begin to fade the moment
the man leaves the clinic unless he pursues a continuous
mode of avoidance of homosexual contact. Pavlov's dog
soon stops salivating if food no longer accompanies the
bell. Sure, someone can give you *temporary* anger or dismay by a cutting remark; they can tell you you're a
hopeless incompetent, and it may get you down; but you'll
only *stay* down if you adopt a mode of self-condemning
actions.

You might in some sense be tricked by someone who
understands self creation if you don't understand it. Mo-

tives are seldom pure and simple; they come in clusters, they have corollaries. A leader talks you into joining the block association with the announced motive of keeping out people who can't afford the taxes; the reasonable-sounding motive in fact entails a series of activities based on the belief that blacks don't belong in the neighborhood. The result is that unwittingly you build your own prejudice against blacks. A leader says, "Do this to save our banking and currency system"—and the effect is to build prejudice against the Jews. A leader says, "Burn down those three particular stores that charge gougingly high prices"; all three are owned by whites, and soon Whitey seems fair game. We are enticed to circumvent the law to achieve some particular good, without noticing that one of the effects is to undermine respect for law in general. We're invited to suppress facts to save our leader from what seems like an undeniably heinous and unjustified conspiracy to get him; but what's also being reinforced is the more general passion to protect the leader against *any* attack. The clever leader can concoct a series of ruses—situations where we pursue a particular unimpeachable good—that entices us to adopt general attitudes that we never would have chosen to embrace if we knew at the outset what we were doing to ourselves.

In *For Whom the Bell Tolls*, Ernest Hemingway tells how Pablo seduces a placid townfolk into generating hatred of fascists. The people know some fascists, but as neighbors or owners of their land, not as enemies. Pablo rounds up a dozen fascists, puts them in a shack, and then arms the townspeople with flails and scythes and other instruments. He lines the townspeople up in two long rows between the shack and the edge of a cliff. The first fascist is marched out between the rows of peasants. He goes past the first few with none of them striking him. But finally one, who had been a tenant on his land, smashes him on the side of the head, and the rest join in. They toss him off the edge of the cliff. There is greater readiness to club the next fascist when he comes out. More of the peasants join in. Soon the peasants hate the fascists for whatever behavior they display, for erectness of gait, for silence, for talking, for disdain, for pride; and they kill with relish:

> There was blood now on their hands and on their clothing, and now began to be the feeling that those who came out were truly enemies and should be killed.

Beware of anyone who is enticing you to act in an unaccustomed mode. Be sure of the effects on you of the new mode, by being sure of the motives it will be honoring. Life-styles can very quickly create their own momentum. That's a peril when you don't understand the self creation principle. But when you do understand it, it's an exhilarating reason for hope.

HOW TO MAKE A COMPLAINT **12**

Okay, there's someone in your life who does a specific thing that you feel you have a legitimate right to complain about. How do you do it? What follows here is an adaptation of some pages from an earlier book of mine, *The Action Approach*.

Complaining is an art as well as a responsibility. It's easy to say "Speak up," much easier than it is to speak up; and it's easier to speak up than it is to make an objection in a way that is fair and forceful and accurate. Like any art, that of making objections takes practice, and following new principles may feel unnatural at first.

Working with married couples over the years, I've evolved a set of suggestions, and have been astounded at how rapidly they've helped communication in many relationships. If you and someone else are quarreling regularly, I strongly suggest that you try them out. Perhaps you won't want to adopt them permanently, but they are very likely to bring peace for a time, during which you may decide which of them are helpful. I shall also make suggestions about how to accept a complaint. If the person to whom you make your objections is willing to follow them, your job will be easier; and if the two of you are willing to adopt both sets on a provisional basis, I think you will soon learn much about the source of the trouble between you. You may consider it a worthy plan to follow all the ground rules to be presented, in all your relationships. Making them habitual may help avoid many kinds of confusion.

1. **Complain to the person you think is harming you, and not to anyone else.**
2. **Try not to object to your mate's behavior in front of anyone else.** To most people, being criticized feels like being personally attacked. Criticism is so often used as a vehicle for personal assault that it is not surprising they associate the two. Your indifference to your mate's comfort displayed by your willingness to criticize him in front of others will be taken at least as seriously as the content of what you say. In fairness to him and for you own sake, unless waiting would be costly for some special reason, wait till you are alone with him. Your mate deserves the chance to make his own impressions on people, without the shadow of your evaluations of him. This means that you're also doing him harm by praising him in front of other people.
3. **Don't compare the person's behavior with that of other people.** Tell a woman that your former wife, Jane, wouldn't have kept you waiting so long, and you're almost sure to start a fight. No one wants to be described as inferior to anyone else. Comparisons will nearly always predispose other people not to listen to what you say, even where the complaint you want to make is jusitfied.

    Anyhow, comparisons of this kind are always irrelevant. Our standard for our own

performance must not be based on what
other people do, but on what we believe we
can do. Therefore, the attempt to whip
someone into submission by comparing him
with other people misses the point. And beware of implied comparisons, like those con-
veyed by expressing disappointment with
someone. The disappointing person is being
compared with his better self.

4. **Make your complaint as soon as you can;
   that is, as soon as you're alone with the
   other person and can articulate it.** Speaking
   up, like any task, becomes more difficult
   when you postpone it. Waiting allows your
   anger to build, and increases the likelihood
   that you'll make irrelevant comments. If you
   criticize someone for what he did long ago,
   you will look like a brooder. The impression
   will be accurate, and the other person will
   feel less comfortable with you afterwards.

5. **Don't repeat a point once you've made it
   and the other person has carefully considered it.** This means, don't expect a signed
   confession after you've spoken. The reward
   for patiently listening to criticism ought to
   be exoneration from having to hear the same
   crime discussed again. A person's action
   against you either warrants ending the relationship with him, or it doesn't. If it doesn't,
   be a sport! Don't keep reminding him of
   whatever you think he did wrong, once you
   have brought the act to his attention and
   told him your reactions.

   I've worked with couples who had spent
   years rehashing each other's violations of
   their relationship; and they repeated their
   arguments, almost word for word as before,

in my office. Usually I suggest a statute of limitations according to which each person can make whatever objections he wants to, but make them only once. He must make them within twenty-four hours of the offense, the time to be counted from when the two people are alone. As days go by, they must reduce the time interval when objections are allowable, until it is as little as a half-hour. Objections which have not been voiced during the allowable period become null and void after it. The plan has two immediate advantages. It forces people to verbalize objects by taking away their reward for being silent; it gives to people who are unsure whether they've offended the knowledge that after a given time interval they need not fear rebuke.

Nearly always, the people who've been arguing accept my recommendation immediately, not realizing how heavily they've depended on citing other people's abuses of them as a way of defending themselves. When trouble erupts between them, both of them feel bereft of requisite weapons. Either they break their pact, or wait for the other person to break it, and then they barrage him with their store of references to his past. Practice is needed to resist this temptation. However, when two people can manage to desist from referring to one another's past as an argumentative device, they frequently discover that they don't have enough information left to sustain arguments like those that kept them up late into the night.

6. **Object only to actions that the other person**

can change. Your comments will be constructive only if they pertain to behavior the other person can change. You may ask a person not to shout, but if you ask him not to be angry with you, you're probably asking too much. I always ask patients who wear sunglasses to take them off in my office, both for their sakes and for mine, since I can make better contact with people when I can see their eyes. But though nervousness is often the reason that these people come to my office with sunglasses, it would be pointless for me to ask them to relax.

Always remember that you may object only to *behavior*. You may ask that your mate get new eyeglasses, but you may not criticize him because his eyes are deteriorating with age. You may object to his leaving dirty clothing scattered about the house, but not to his being too short. If he cannot change it by an act of will, it's not a legitimate subject for complaint.

7. **Make your complaints vocally, not facially.** A yawn has ended many a party, and a handdog look has made many a husband wonder what he did wrong. Certain employers are experts at looking downcast when even their most dedicated workers decide that it's time to go home. At the end of a ten-hour workday, when you walk past one of them on your way to the door, he may look at you sadly, as though you've broken an intimate pact with him.

Facial expressions sometimes succeed in getting people to do what they don't want to do, but we don't look forward to meeting the people who bully us by sighing or acting disappointed with us. The fact that the victims of facial expressions seldom identify the tactic being used against them is undoubtedly what commends the tactic to its users. After a while, though, the user loses awareness of how he is influencing other people, and his face becomes his misfortune.

Facial expressions of all kinds are outward complements of the spirit. Our expressions may be rich and various, but they cease to be when we use them as devices to convey messages we are reluctant to put into words.

8. **Try to make only one complaint at a time.** If you make more, you'll demoralize the other person, and perhaps obscure your major point. Don't quibble about the carpeting in your office when you've stormed in to ask your boss for a well-deserved promotion. If the subject changes to the price of carpets you'll feel unsatisfied; and your boss may feel he's discharged his obligation by promising to have your carpet changed.

9. **Don't preface your complaint.** "Listen. There's something I've wanted to tell you for a long time. It may hurt you badly, but please don't feel offended by what I'm going to say. . . ."

"I want to tell you something, and it's for your own good. Now listen carefully to what I'm going to say. . . ."

What could be worse than a preface like either of these? Instead of inoculating your listener against the pain of what you are going to tell him, you are stabbing him to death with your hypodermic needle. By prefaces, you convince both him and yourself that your complaint is to be monstrous and that probably he won't be capable of receiving it with the same friendly spirit that you feel while making it. There are perhaps as many people killed by prefaces as by complaints.

10. **Don't apologize for your complaint after making it.** Telling the person you're sorry you had to disagree with him is apologizing for what you said in good faith. Apologizing is asking the other perpson to brace you so that you won't fall down under the stress of disagreeing with him. Doing so imposes an unnecessary burden on him; it will detract from the merit of your accomplishment in your own mind and renew your conflict about whether you had the right to say what you did.

11. **Avoid sarcasm.** Among the invariable motivations for sarcasm are contempt and fear. Your contempt will predispose the other person not to heed you, and because you are making a choice not to confront him directly, you are intensifying your fear of him. Being sarcastic is sniveling, no matter how clever your turn of phrase. Sarcastic people have no dignity. They are cowards.

12. **Don't ask people *why* they're doing something to which you object. Ask them to stop, if that is the underlying idea you wish to express.** "Why are you interrupting me?" "Why are you putting your feet on my chair?" It's obvious in each case that the speaker wants the other person to stop an activity. Probably he doesn't feel strong enough to make the request openly. He cloaks it as a scientific inquiry. The question is worse than an inaccurate articulation of

what is wanted. It would be easier for the other person to stop what he's doing than to search for his motivation and report it accurately to you. Many people regard serious questions about their motivations as obnoxious invasions of their privacy.

13. **Rehearse your presentation if you need to.**

14. **Don't talk about other people's motivations when objecting to an activity.** Tell them simply what they are doing; and, if it is relevant, why you feel they ought not do it. Here are examples of statements that are objectionable because they include irrelevant speculations about the motives of the offender:

"You never *want* me to finish what I'm saying."

"You *don't care* how long I wait for you."

"Quit *trying* to make me angry."

If you stop playing psychoanalyst with people, and tell them how they're offending without giving them diagnoses, they'll become much more receptive to what you say. Each of the statements mentioned runs an unnecessary risk. It gives the listener reason to disregard your essential complaint if he concludes that your speculation about his motive is wrong.

Statements like these are irritating invasions of the listener's privacy. Hardly a man is now alive who doesn't feel the difference between, "Please don't interrupt me," and "You never want me to finish what I'm saying."

Look out for the tendency to confuse consequence and intention. The fact that someone is stepping on your foot doesn't logically imply that his intention was to hurt you. It may have been. But it may not. Ascribing to people uncanny power which they are supposedly using to harm us is a dangerous practice. This was precisely the assumption made in previous centuries to justify the burning of people as demons and witches.

15. **Avoid words like *always* and *never*; they contain implicit references to the past.** Exaggerations intended for emphasis when making an objection rob you of accuracy, and of all the psychological advantages that go with it.

16. **If you never compliment the other person, don't expect him to remain open to your criticisms.** There was supposedly a little girl who didn't talk till she was eight. Doctors, social workers, and psychiatrists were all consulted but couldn't figure out why. Then one day at breakfast she cried out, "This oatmeal is lumpy." When asked why she had never spoken before, she answered that up till then everything had been all right.

Don't be this little girl. Complaints ring loud and long when they're the only sounds that are made. If you want to make occasional objections, you have the obligation to compliment the person at other times. And I recommend the practice of thanking people for listening to your criticisms.

TAKE CRITICISM HOW TO **13**

You're going to need criticism from other people as long as you live. Especially from those who want the best for you. You know you're not infallible, but if criticism hurts too much, you may find yourself pretending you are. It is crucial to your happiness that you learn how to take criticism—for your own sake and for the sake of others.

Even if there is someone else in your life who is riddled with shortcomings and who clashes with you regularly, don't be trapped into arguing for or believing in your own perfection.

Since everyone is wrong sometimes, the thing to do is learn *how* to be wrong. If you don't, you're likely to start avoiding criticism. And as soon as you start to avoid something, you also start to fear it.

Few people really want to be criticized. Many have cultivated devices to ward it off. They have an agonizing sense of fear whenever anyone finds fault with them. Out of this fear they stay away from experiences where they might get criticized. You take too easy a job, perhaps, or find a lover who won't ask much of you. But it's not only the loss of experience that matters; the criticism itself could have been useful. Some of us half acknowledge this by fighting off every critic—but secretly listening to what they say. "Don't be ridiculous, Jack, no one minds if I take two hours or so for lunch." Still, you somehow start cutting back on the lunch hours. But next time Jack may not be willing to tell you what he thinks. Or to talk to you, if he's afraid you'll snap his head off. Fear or anger at criticism can stifle your friendships as well as deprive you of good advice.

The irony of it. You're afraid that your flaws will disqualify you for love or success, so you try to hide them. And the deception increases your fear. We can see the paranoid elements at work in a fear of criticism. As soon as you hear someone say, "By the way, you made a mistake . . . ," you're sure that he's seen through you and knows all your secret flaws. If the would-be critic is a friend, and the friendship collapses, you'll probably blame those flaws for turning him against you. When more likely it was your style of warding off criticism. It's a never-ending cycle—as long as you keep avoiding criticism. The next friend who makes any adverse comment—even the mildest, most familiar complaint—will seem to be turning against you too.

The only way to stop this cycle is to start facing, even encouraging, criticism. Telling yourself that you'll listen to it the next time isn't enough; you have to learn to recognize the many ways you've developed of *not* listening. For example:

1. **Don't shout at the critic and then get up and leave.**
2. **Don't interrupt to argue without hearing him out.**
3. **Under no condition find fault with him— in an effort to disqualify him as a judge.** "You should talk! What about the time you. . . ." Don't correct his bad grammar or irrelevant factual errors.
4. **Don't act catastrophic.** Don't start wailing,

"I'm worthless," or "I always make a mess of things."

5. **Don't beg off on the grounds of not being emotionally strong enough to handle criticism.** Don't create the impression that the other person is destroying your spirit. Don't be a fragile bully.

6. **Don't blame someone else for your own actions.** "If you hadn't asked me to go with you to that party I wouldn't have spent so much money on clothes this afternoon."

7. **Don't change the subject, as if you didn't hear the criticism.**

8. **Don't repeat over and over that you're sorry, without ever showing that you understood the criticism.** This technique can be quite subtle; the critic's sure that you didn't hear him, but finds it hard to say so as long as you're busy apologizing.

9. **Don't shift the conversation to the reasons *why* you acted as you did.** Again: this can be subtle. Your critic may think at the time that you're dealing with the criticism, but later he has this strange feeling of having been bypassed.

10. **Don't criticize the other person's reaction to your behavior.** For instance, don't call him oversensitive or impossible to please. *His* reaction is not the point.

11. **Don't jest.** Flippancy is properly perceived as contemptuous by a great many people, and is hurtful to everyone.

12. **Don't imply that your critic has some ulterior, hostile motive for making his objection.** If you are asking why the other person has objected to your act, you are not dealing with his objection. The question about him

should come later, if ever. Perhaps he doesn't know his motive. That fact ought not to deprive him of the right to object to something you do.

13. **Don't caricature the complaint.** If a person says you were *thoughtless*, don't ascribe to him the statement that you were *vicious* and then defend yourself against a charge he didn't make. If he exaggerates, don't seize his exaggeration and take it literally. The deliberate exaggeration of a charge against you amounts to a dismissal of the charge.

Think back to the last time anyone criticized you, and—especially—watch the next time. How many of these avoidance tricks do you use? Make a rule not to use *any* of them from now on, and try the following techniques instead. Remember that it'll be hard at first to break a long-standing habit, but resisting the use of your own defenses will quickly make you feel stronger.

1. **Listen to what the critic says without speaking at first.** Don't use your face or body in any way to discourage the critic. Look directly at him to convey your willing reception.

2. **Rephrase the criticism (in your own mind) in terms of ways you choose to act.** If the critic is deriding you for being poor or having acne, he's not giving you any useful information. But before you conclude that, look for voluntary actions that you could change the next time around.

3. **Use your intelligence to help articulate the objection, not to obscure it.** After giving a speech at Columbia University, Bertrand Russell was answering questions from the

audience. One student's question brought him to a full stop. For a whole minute he said nothing, his hand over his chin, in thought. Then he peered at the student and rephrased the question, making it sharper and more precise. He asked the student, "Would you say that this is still your question?" and the student answered delightedly, "Yes." Again Lord Russell thought, this time even longer, nodding his head and twice seeming about to speak. Then looking toward the student, who was in a row far behind me, he said, "That's a very good question, young man. I don't believe I can answer it." A demonstration by a genius of how to use one's intelligence to help someone find a possible flaw in one's own reasoning! The reward: the discovery of the flaw.

The student who posed the question, a young philosophy instructor, was a hero afterward. I remember him smiling as he walked out of the auditorium surrounded by colleagues. But could he have done what Lord Russell did? And to what extent is genius composed of abilities like the one Lord Russell demonstrated?

4. **Try asking the critic politely what you could have done differently, and why it would have been better.** Ask this not in an attempt to catch him out, but to understand him and to learn alternative conduct that, when you evaluate it objectively, you may accept as preferable.

5. **Clarify for yourself, even if the critic doesn't tell you, what harm the criticized act did—to you, to your critic, or to anyone else.** (If you can't find *any* harm in it, the

critic may be out of bounds. I'll talk more later about ways you can be sure.)

6. **Whether or not you agree with the criticism, let your critic know that you heard and understood it.** Restate the criticism in your own words—not simply repeating the words he used. Parroting your critic's words is a common device to feign listening when you really haven't been.

7. **Mention the way your critic *reported* feeling.** Not how you think he should feel or how you'd have felt. "I'm sorry you felt lonely and embarrassed waiting for me at the restaurant. I can see how bad it was."

8. **If you think the criticism is unwarranted, say so only *after* hearing him out and following these rules.** You'll still feel sorry, perhaps, that your critic suffered. Even if *he* got the time wrong and was at the restaurant an hour early, the experience was unpleasant. But this is your chance to explain the situation as you see it.

9. **On the other hand, if you agree you were wrong and are willing to try not to repeat the mistake, say you're sorry.** But say it once, at most twice; don't beg forgiveness over and over. The humiliation involved in that can increase rather than soothe your dread of criticism.

10. **If only a few people dare to criticize you—whether because you're a big shot or because you've been known to turn nasty—do what you can to encourage those few.** Thank anyone who offers honest criticism.

You may want to add to this list. And you may want to use the magnification involved in this process to learn more about your fears. Ask yourself these questions as you start listening to criticism: "What weakness in me is being revealed?" "What happens next—how will my critic treat me?" "Does this experience remind me in any way of my past? If so, how was I helpless then but not now?"

When Catherine's husband Doug told her she'd offended a guest at their party, she was sure he no longer loved her. This feeling grew more intense when she stopped herself from shouting at him and storming out of the room. As she asked herself why, she realized that she saw her contribution to the marriage as a perfect social style. In her six years with Doug, she'd refused to face any social mistakes, and she has since learned that they do not cause fury, that doing her best is all that matters.

It's especially important to be receptive to critics who have nothing at all to gain—and possibly something to lose. An operating room nurse on a new job tells a famous surgeon that one of his instruments isn't sterile. A friend who knows you're touchy on the subject tells you you're driving dangerously. Whether they're right or wrong—and it's possible they didn't understand some aspect of things —their intentions are likely to be good. They're trying to prevent real harm.

This is the kind of criticism you need, so don't oppose it even if the critic *is* wrong in some particular case. The next time he may see something important that you've overlooked.

Stan, a successful young salesman, came to see me because his success made him nervous. He was especially nervous about criticism. He'd done so well, he knew he didn't deserve it . . . and criticism would mean the critic recognized that. After a few months of reversing his old avoidance habits, he was no longer afraid that every critic was about to face him with the ugly truth—in fact, he wasn't so sure there *was* an ugly truth. But one thing bothered him.

"This man I work with criticizes me *all* the time.

'Where'd you dig up that accent? Who taught *you* manners?' Over and over. I can't take it. He's not trying to help—and I can't believe it's helping me to put up with it."

Stan's right. *Some* people who criticize you are just taking out their frustration, jealousy, whatever. You don't have to be a doormat for them to walk on. But, as we've seen, the answer isn't to shy away from all criticism. It's to learn what your rights are—and aren't.

As long as you won't give critics a chance, as long as you'll yell, cry, attack, do anything to keep from listening, you can't very well ask them to give *you* a chance. To keep their comments constructive and reasonable. But once you're willing, in the ways I've outlined above, to give critics a fair hearing, you're entitled to ask certain things in return.

Insist, first of all, that all criticism pertain to things you *do*, not to qualities or facts you can't control. You're never obliged to subject yourself to criticism of your height or age or race. In learning to tolerate criticism, you need to *un*learn the fear of being torn to pieces by it. Knowing that most critics don't try to do anything of the kind—and that the ones who do aren't justified—can help.

Next, try to get a critic to talk about a single act—not to bring up a whole list of past wrongdoings to document his case. It's much easier to listen to criticism if it's not a long and hopeless catalog of everything you've ever done wrong, and a well-meaning critic should respect this.

Finally, ask your critic not to repeat what he's said once you've shown that you understand it. And you may ask a critic not to tell you your faults in public.

All these requests are reasonable; still, you may not always get your way. If the boss wants to stand in the hall and tell you three times how you fouled up his project, there isn't too much you can do about it. Except to recognize that he isn't so much criticizing as attacking, and is probably taking out his own tensions. Even if he was right the first time, he's not right the third. Abuse like this is not the nature of the beast, criticism; it's more the nature of your boss. And if scenes like this happen often, you might want to start looking for a new job.

You can identify the vicious critics by their response when you ask them to be specific and moderate or after you hear them out. If you've honestly considered their criticism, and they refuse to forgive your mistakes, then those mistakes were never the real issue. These critics have it in for you or perhaps for everybody. As long as you respond gracefully to criticism, you'll know that you're offering critics all reasonable access to you, and it's their problem if they refuse it.

At the same time, be careful not to give others the same kind of trouble. Don't criticize anyone for ulterior reasons—to show your superiority or vent your anger over something unrelated. It's hard to learn that criticism and contempt don't have to go together if you yourself combine them.

When was the last time anyone criticized you? If it's been a while, you've probably been guarding against it in some way—which has intensified your fear. But resolve, next time, to be ready to listen. Once you find that criticism doesn't have to destroy your confidence, friendships, or career, you can go a long way toward improving all three.

FRIENDS AND LOVERS: EIGHT QUESTIONS TO ASK YOURSELF **14**

Up to now I've talked about how you make yourself the way you are, and how you can make yourself over. But what about relationships with other people? Can the Principle help to make them richer, more honest, more satisfying?

Yes, because your feeling about anyone is reinforced every time you do something prompted by that feeling. If you dislike someone now, then disparaging him and trying to ruin his reputation will make you despise him even more. If you love someone and act lovingly you will sustain that love and make it grow. Trust someone, and you'll come to believe he's trustworthy unless he does something extreme. Start checking up on him and, unless the evidence is overwhelmingly in his favor, you will become still more suspicious. The beginning of the end in many relationships is when one partner starts secretly writing down his complaints, compiling a dossier. I don't recommend compiling *favorable* dossiers either, but the chances of a compiler's performing a loving act are higher after writing a complimentary entry than after a damning entry, and if it's a fundamentally good relationship that the compiler wants to preserve through a troubled patch, favorable dossiers are better than unfavorable ones: not as documents but as activities.

The examples are endless. Treating others with respect is one of the best ways to make yourself feel that human beings—yourself included—are worthy of respect and dignity.

"Yet each man kills the thing he loves," wrote Oscar Wilde. We don't always know *how* to act lovingly, *how* to treat everyone with respect. Or we don't recognize the true effect, on ourselves and on our relationships, of our actions.

Every month new books, new magazine articles appear giving advice on how to handle yourself in relationships. How to get people to respect you, promote you in jobs, find you sexy, or love you. Success is measured by the kind of response you elicit—whether you do, in fact, get people to respect you, promote you in jobs, and so on. The goal is to understand what makes people respond to you, so that you can package yourself in the most appealing way possible.

But the response in others is not nearly so important as the response in yourself. The Principle is always true, always in operation when you act. And so the things you do to attract other people into respecting you and giving you what you want are also affecting your self-image. Which means that you may succeed—you may get the admiration you want from another person—and actually like yourself *less* for it.

The idea that your self-image is created from the appraisals other people make of you has gone unexamined far too long. We all know examples of people who are successful and widely respected but nonetheless loathe themselves. There are people like this who commit suicide. Yet there are other people, with few friends and many enemies, who somehow manage to sustain optimism and self-confidence.

Good appraisals from others are worthless if you can't

believe them, if you have a low opinion of yourself. And the most coveted job or desired lover can't make you happy if you're suffering some private torment. As we've seen, you can create a deep personal problem like depression or paranoia in the course (and often in the name) of building a relationship. Some tactics can destroy the very bond they were meant to seal.

In fact, *anything you do for the sake of a relationship that also makes you dislike yourself will eventually harm that relationship.* You'll feel resentment, or the other person will lose respect for you, or perhaps you'll become so anxious that the relationship isn't worth it. One way or another, your suffering will hurt the relationship. And there's no need for this. Instead, you have to find out how your actions are affecting *you*—and how they're affecting the way you feel about people you care about. You can find out by asking yourself these eight questions.

1. *Am I overinhibiting myself in the relationship?* For instance, you may stop yourself from seeing certain friends, from doing particular things, from mentioning subjects that remain important to you. You do this out of love or consideration—you don't want to displease the other person. But you feel cheated. You are catering to the other person more than you want to, and someday it will make you depressed or angry. And you are generating a tension within yourself, a sense of fragility in the relationship that is damaging.

2. *Am I acting toward the other person in ways that will cause me to dislike him or her?* Maybe you lie to your mate: "I'll be out shopping all afternoon, dear," when you're actually going to a movie. The lie can affect *you* —it can make you anxious or guilty—but it can also affect the way you view your mate.

"Man, is he gullible—believing that shopping story the third time in a row! He must be stupid, or maybe he just doesn't care."

Even small lies can change your attitude toward another person. For instance, a man I know vowed to give up smoking. He and his wife counted the days since he'd last had a cigarette and went out to dinner to celebrate after each week. They shared a sense of camaraderie and triumph. But then he began smoking again and decided not to tell her. By the subterfuge he convinced himself that she was a hard, narrow person who tried to deny him privileges. He cast her in the role of unpleasant authority and so taught himself to like her less. And the more general idea you're reinforcing by lying is that if your partner knew you for what you really are she or he would despise you.

3. *Do I ridicule the other person?* You might, for example, feel unhappy that you and your wife have a limited education or income. When you're with people you want to impress, you start to criticize your wife—to be snide or apologetic about her. Which has two effects: First, you increase your sense that your own limitations are crippling; and second, by turning your own conflict into contempt for another person, you teach yourself to see her as a symbol of what is wrong with your own life.

4. *Am I pretending to be someone I'm not because of this person?* Perhaps you try to act sophisticated. You pretend you hold attitudes about sex that actually make you uncomfortable. Or you go along with the person when he acts in ways you consider unfair. He

chooses snobs as friends or laughs at unfortunate people, and you act as if you approved in order to avoid conflict. Whenever the motivation is some apparent benefit to you (making you seem more attractive, shielding you from trouble) pretense is harmful, not beneficial.

5. *Am I putting the person on a pedestal?* You assume he can do no wrong. You're sure everyone must find him attractive, witty, impressive—so sure that you rarely examine your real feelings. And so you're more intent on contributing to his support system than you are on being honest. In the end this means that you are inviting him to act toward you in ways that are damaging both to his vision of you and your own vision of yourself.

6. *Am I putting pressure on the person to change his usual way of life?* Do you want him to stop seeing friends you don't like or to join the bridge club with you even though he's never liked the game? Or to dress differently, talk differently, get a better job? If the person gives in to you without really wanting to, he may well be storing up resentment.

There may be some advice—such as Rachel's suggestion to Phil that he stop bragging—that is extremely helpful, perhaps even essential to the relationship, and it must be given. But always remember that there is a risk to it. Meantime you're reinstating the idea that he is not good enough for you as he is.

7. *Am I allowing the person to mistreat me on the premise that these things don't matter if the relationship is good?* Your friend is inconsiderate; she makes jokes at your expense in

front of people. You don't want to make a fuss and so hold still for this treatment. What you don't realize is that the other person is teaching herself in this way to lose respect for you. Henry Ford's line explains: "A man will never forgive you for the wrongs he has done to you." And you're undermining your own sense of worth by acting on the premise that abuse of you is okay.

8. *Do I have different standards of behavior for myself and my mate?* Your husband gets furious if you interrupt him at work or contradict his opinions. But if you object when he does the same to you, he jokes about your oversensitivity. Or perhaps you're the one who demands respectful treatment but doesn't give it. In either case, you are injecting resentment into the relationship, and you're reinstating the degrading idea that the two of you don't deserve equal respect.

In addition to these eight questions, ask yourself: "How do I behave or talk differently when I'm with the person (employer, friend, lover) from the way I do when he's absent?" The answer will give you important clues about compromises you may be making, or devices you may be using, or pretenses you may be adopting.

Every "yes" answer to the eight questions above is a danger signal; it means you're acting in ways that can hurt you and hurt your love and trust for another person. This is true even if the relationship *looks* just fine, even if outsiders think that you have the perfect life with your mate.

Try to look at it this way instead. When you start out, the trouble probably isn't all that serious. If you talk about it, if you get in the habit of giving and taking reasonable criticism, there's a good chance that you and your partner will work things out. Better than a good chance. But if you choose to avoid the problem, you keep making that problem worse. It gets to seem more important, more complicated, more fearsome than it needs to be. And you make yourself less compatible with the person who's part of that problem.

The rule is, any acts that would tend to produce bad feelings in *you*—rage, depression, self-loathing, whatever—aren't good for your relationships either. Everything I've said in this book about the importance of trying *never* to act out of fear is critical with someone you love. A loving relationship is too valuable a part of your life to let it erode unnecessarily.

HOW TO LOVE 15

You've been in love; you know what it's like. It's a sense of delight, not just in the person you love, but in all people, in yourself, in life. Suddenly you see beauty, excitement everywhere. You're not afraid to express your love: passionately, gently, in words, or in silence. And you feel strong, generous, fully alive.

But something always happens. Maybe you've only been able to love for a few minutes or a few weeks—until you saw the person walk away with someone else. Or maybe you've loved someone who died. Or somehow you seemed to "fall out of love" every time.

Now you've more or less given up. You *seem* to have loving relationships; you're married, or you have a lover, or you've had a hundred lovers. Or you're sure that you love your friends, your parents, your children as much as anyone. But in fact you've been stung, confused, disappointed once too often. You're just not going to get that involved anymore.

Some of us do this on purpose. We've been hurt, so we've talked ourselves out of believing in love. "What good is it, anyway?" We've decided to withdraw and become practical. Our friends have to be useful to us, our marriages "sensible." Love, we can see now, is for children —and we're growing up, facing reality.

Others of us *want* to love but can't seem to express our feelings. Harold's wife Celia told me that the most important thing in the world to him was seeing his grandchildren. When he knew they were coming to visit, he'd be happy and eager all day. "What's keeping them?" he'd ask every five minutes when they were late. But as soon as everyone got there, he'd go inside the house, leaving Celia alone to greet them. When the children played in the yard, he'd watch them through the window; he wouldn't say much to them even after they came indoors. Celia would explain that he'd been working hard and was tired. And Harold would wonder why he was so depressed at the end of every visit.

"Why does he keep doing that?" their son asked Celia. "He gets upset if we don't come and visit, and then he doesn't even talk to us."

Harold keeps doing this because—he thinks—he has no choice. He's old; what can he say to these kids who are sixty years younger? What can he possibly share with them? You can't expect him to join them in games of tag in the yard. . . .

One way or another, those of us who don't know how to love—and most of us could learn how to love more fully—have excuses, ways of blaming it all on fate. "I just haven't found the right person." "Everyone keeps walking out on me." "Whenever I get interested in someone, I always find out they already have someone else."

But it isn't fate that keeps us from loving; it's our own attitudes: toward love, toward other people, and toward ourselves. And these attitudes, like any other attitude, can be changed through our actions.

HOW TO TAP FEELINGS OF LOVE

Act lovingly when you feel like it. We all have feelings of love or warmth for someone at some time. But we don't act on them. And so the Principle goes to work:

every time we hold back from expressing love, we make ourselves more afraid to express it or even believe in it. But we can reverse this cycle. If we can only begin to act on love when we feel it, we can teach ourselves to be giving, receptive, and unafraid.

"When we feel it" is all-important. The Principle says that we reinforce our motives by acting on them. Which means that I can't make myself love someone I now can't stand simply by acting as if I loved him. But I *can* intensify a love I already feel by acting on it.

So the place to start is with someone you love, or sometimes love. It can be your mate or a lover or relative or an old friend who's glad to see you. There's only one requirement—that you have moments when you feel you love this person. And then you can go to work reinforcing those feelings instead of suppressing them. It's *not* up to fate. As Wordsworth put it,

> And you must love him, ere to you
> He will seem worthy of your love.

What if you're not even sure that you love the person? Well, spend a few minutes imagining. Picture yourself in the world without him. You'll never see him again. What did you leave unsaid? "Thanks"? "I'm sorry"? "I love you"? What will be missing in your life from now on? Your friend's smile? The good times? The company, the intelligence, the sensuality, the hope, the energy? Define it for yourself. If you love the person at all, you'll find a lot of answers. And simply taking the time to think about what you value in a person can begin to strengthen your love.

But the best way to strengthen love is through *acts* of love. An act of love is an act with no other purpose—a pure expression of feeling that is not disguised in any way. Jeremy called his wife at work the other day when he was feeling warm toward her. "I just wanted to hear the sound of your voice. Have you got time for us to talk?"

That was an act of love. It was honest, direct, emotional. Compare it with Alan's call to *his* wife. "Hi. I just wanted to know if everything was all right."

Alan has felt estranged from his wife for some time, and he's trying to move closer to her. But he doesn't admit that is why he is calling. His motives are actually mixed; he does want to express some feeling for his wife, but not at the risk of losing his cool. So his tone stays detached, a bit condescending. And his fear of emotional contact— which *might* make him lose his cool—gets reinforced by his action.

Suppose you buy someone a present. When you give it to him, you can say, "I got you this because I thought you could use it." Or you can say—if it's true—"I got you this because I was thinking how great you are." If both are true, saying the second will almost surely make you a more loving person.

We give presents for all kinds of reasons, and probably each statement has a place in life. But the pure expression of feeling—assuming the feeling is there—will help to strengthen your love. If you love someone and don't say so, you're not only cheating the other person; you're cheating yourself out of a capacity to feel.

If you want to know what to say about your love for someone, ask yourself, once again, what you'd miss if that person were no longer there. Be as specific as possible. This may take some thought; most of us aren't really used to putting our love into words. But *find* the words: an honest statement of the way you feel. Rehearse that statement if you wish; tell yourself, "When I have that certain rush of feeling, I will say _____." Then, when the time comes, say it. Take a chance. You'll feel more vulnerable than you are used to feeling, and you will feel more loving.

Harold, the grandfather just mentioned, broke this process down into several stages. The first was to talk to his grandchildren, not necessarily to express feelings, but to force himself not to withdraw completely. Then he started looking for activities he could share with them, telling the children, "I don't really know your games; let's find one we can all play," and eventually adding, "so that I don't feel left out." After a number of visits, he found himself saying "I missed you" when they arrived and going on to talk about his other feelings and experiences.

A statement describing how you *felt,* as in "I missed you," won't be as effective in overcoming the fear of love as one revealing how you feel *now*: "I feel very close to you now." But the one about the past may be easier to say at first. It's worthwhile—any disclosure of warm feelings can help you to make a start.

The following suggestions are almost sure to make you more loving:

1. **Make a special occasion of some activity that you and the other person now do together mechanically.** First, pick something you don't think about much, but just hurry through: perhaps eating breakfast together or talking over the day's events or making love. Then slow down. Try giving twice the time—or more—to that activity. Savor it. This is good for the relationship, and it's good for your attitude about love: When you give it time, you reinforce your sense of its value.

2. **Give the person you love something *perishable.*** Something the person likes. Maybe you think it's throwing away money to buy flowers or feed a jukebox. But it's not. It's a gift for both of you. When you want to do something for that person, spend your money there —not on a book you think he or she should read.

   This doesn't mean that you'll destroy your love if you ever buy someone a useful present. But try to be a little impractical once in a while; it can help you to realize that love is always worthwhile in itself—even if nothing should come of it.

3. **Express your affection by touch.** Many of us are inhibited about touching others except to initiate sex. Which always means that we're a bit inhibited about expressing feelings. Sex is wonderful, but also make sure that you touch the person you love simply to express affection.

4. **Be careful not to assign the person a role that makes it harder for you to love him or her.** Roy always lets his wife play the heavy, telling him when he's had enough to drink at a party and when it's time to go home. He acts like a teen-ager and casts his wife as angry parent—which can only undermine his love for her.

You can't really love someone if you make him or her your conscience. Angela was ashamed of herself for being overweight, but that wasn't how she explained the situation to her friends. "I've got to go on a diet, or else my husband will hate me." So she began to resent her husband ("Why can't he love me the way I am?"), when in fact she was the one who really minded the extra weight. Note that this is distinguished from trying to improve yourself in order to give pleasure to your mate; the distinction hinges on whether or not you impute active current disapproval to him. If you do something to give pleasure to someone, you build warmth; if you do it to avoid disapproval, you build fear.

5. **Think about the person's flaws that trouble**

you most. Then ask yourself, "Do I have the same flaws, or am I afraid of getting them?" If so, face the problem in yourself. Even before you find a solution, this honest appraisal can free you to love the person.

Max hated to look at his wife's face as she got older. He wanted to live forever, and her wrinkles reminded him that he was not going to make it. By complaining all the time about her clothes, her gray hair, her make-up, he destroyed much of his love for her. Only when he realized that getting old was his own fear—and began to take action to wipe out that fear—was he able to love her again.

6. **Most of all, do something (preferably many things) you love doing with the person.** What it is doesn't matter: a picnic, a trip, an evening at the theater, a game of Scrabble at home. Try to remember things you once enjoyed sharing—and do them again in spite of all the reasons you think you can't. Find ways to see each other in a better light, to associate pleasure and fulfillment with each other. Study how you act, how free you are, when you are happy together, even for an afternoon. And do more things together in the same vein.

These are only suggestions; the specific words and actions you use to express your love are best if they come from you. Your emotional involvement will bring originality. The important thing is to *act*; don't just wait for tender moments and then sit through them passively. You can get all sentimental listening to old records, but it won't make you more able to love unless you do something to reinforce the feeling. Besides, according to Shakespeare,

"They do not love that do not show their love." In order to love, you've got to act lovingly.

BUT I'M AFRAID . . .

Old habits are hard to break. If you're not used to expressing warmth openly, you're likely to be shy about it. You'll feel foolish, vulnerable, out of character. It isn't easy to say to a friend during a long afternoon, "I really enjoy being with you." It's true—and it would almost certainly mean more to both of you than anything else you've been saying. But it's surprisingly hard to say.

As you start to go against your old habits, you'll set new fears in motion. They'll reveal precious information, if you study them. You can learn from these fears through the method of magnification. You can find out *why* you've been afraid to love—to love this person or to love in general. And you can start overcoming that fear.

When you feel anxious about expressing love, ask yourself:

1. What might I lose by loving this person?
2. What terrible things am I revealing about myself?
3. What power am I giving to the person by expressing myself in this new way?
4. How will the person harm me?
5. In what ways am I foolish to love the person?

What, in other words, are you afraid of? You may discover that you fear:

1. *Being betrayed.* You're afraid that if you reveal your deep fondness for someone, he'll abuse your trust. He'll make demands of you,

take over your life—or he'll walk out completely.

2. *Making a fool of yourself.* You can't talk that
way. It seems preposterous. You're sure the
other person will laugh at you.

3. *Being rejected.* Why should another person
care about how you feel? How can you dare
to think that someone might love you?

4. *Transience.* If you love someone, you will
suffer if you lose him. The idea of his leaving
you—or dying—feels unbearable. It seems better not to experience much of anything than
to risk that amount of pain.

5. *"Melting."* When you express tenderness, it
feels as if you're going to collapse. You'll lose
your freedom, your individuality, maybe even
the use of your arms and legs. You'll dissolve,
you'll melt, you won't be the same person
anymore.

Where do these fears come from? Almost certainly
they come from your own past—from something that happened some time ago that you've turned into a trauma.
You're afraid that you'll be betrayed; perhaps someone,
a parent, betrayed you in the past. Or someone made you
look foolish or walked out on you. Ask yourself who in
the past treated you in the way you're afraid you'll be
treated now.

Describe in words your usual fear when you express
love. Make the description as clear as you can. Get to
understand your secret expectation—for instance, that
you'll "melt" or the love will end. Be ready for it. Know
that the next time you're about to love someone, you'll
hear a voice warning you to turn back. "Don't tell this
person you love her." "Don't act like an idiot." "You'll
lose his respect." "She'll die."

Then disregard the warning. It comes from your past, which doesn't have to repeat itself. If you do your best to express your love in spite of your fears, you'll find that those fears will subside. There are no guarantees. But being willing to make a commitment without any guarantee is what makes love so special.

GETTING THE BEST OUT OF SEX 16

If you want to get more out of sex and to become a better lover, you can't simply concentrate on sexual technique. You have to look at your feelings about sex— your *sexual attitude*. Like all your attitudes, this one is preserved by the way you act. And not merely the way you act with a lover. By the many decisions you make all through your life, you can make yourself receptive to sex—or not. You make yourself a sexual being or a non-sexual one.

Research findings on the sexual drive itself bear out the principle of self creation. If you engage in any kind of sexual activity, then you tend to keep your sex drive high.

But sex, like anything else, tends to lose value for you if you don't pursue it. Not right away. But if you keep placing other things before it, over a period of years, sex takes a lesser place in your mind. Notice I said "placing other things before it." If you're merely deprived through lack of opportunity, your drive may increase. The more important you make sex, the more important it becomes.

But this doesn't mean you should force yourself to have sex so that you can keep your desire high. That won't work. By acting on the wrong motive you can make sex distasteful or limit it over a lifetime.

What is the wrong motive for sex? Anything that is aimed at pleasing someone else—whether that someone is society or your partner—when it *doesn't also please you.*

"SHOULD I SLEEP WITH THIS PERSON NOW?" THREE GUIDELINES

I am going to say three things about sex that may seem surprising or even wrong at first. Yet failing to observe these guidelines has cost more people happy sex lives than anything else they could do.

The first is that *sex isn't necessary.* Better go without sex than misuse it. Bad sex can kill your desire. It can make you dislike your body and make it harder for you to enjoy a good experience later. You need the freedom of knowing that you can say No. As the writer Joanna Fields put it, the essential question of sex is to "ask your body what it would like next."

Watch the damage the opposite approach can do.

Margot had a crush on a man who finally asked her out to dinner. He was late without apologizing, then spent the evening rambling on about the gorgeous women he had known. Clearly Margot wasn't his type—and she was starting to think that he might not be her type either. But when he came up to her apartment later, she didn't say No to sex. And so, she felt dirty when she took her clothes off, was inhibited during intercourse, and got nothing out of it.

The message kept coming to her: This man is not for you—at least not now. But she disregarded it. In trying to ignore her own conflict about him, she brought that conflict into her feelings about sex. It would have been better if she'd postponed sex until she found the courage to confront him about his indifference. Only then, if that went well, could she have gone ahead without conflict and inhibition.

Keep sex feeling like a luxury. Don't let a false

belief in necessity contaminate the experience. The feeling that you *have* to go to bed with someone is disastrous for your outlook on sex.

The final decision about having sex with someone should always be made at the time. Keep the right to say No—so that Yes can have its full value.

Be especially wary of these three common reasons why sex may seem necessary. It *never* is—and you'll help your next sexual experience and future ones by not giving in to these pressures:

(a) *Custom.* "We're married." "I slept with him before." "She expected me to."

(b) *Convenience.* "Maggie is always there." "It'll be cheaper and safer if I move in with Chad." "We might as well."

(c) *Fear of losing someone.* "There's always someone who will if I won't. I never say No if he asks me."

The second guideline is that *sex needn't be orgasmic.* Many couples put themselves under terrible strain by not appreciating this. The man feels responsible for bringing the woman to orgasm; the women feels she's not a real woman unless she has one. Often such couples insist that the orgasm take place during sexual intercourse. Prior sexual acts like kissing or caressing are dismissed as foreplay; the aim is to get on to the big moment—intercourse. Then they judge their future as a couple by how their intercourse goes. It's all a difficult challenge for them, like fighting for some kind of championship.

The simple instruction to do anything, but try *not* to have an orgasm, can often save the sex life of a couple under this kind of strain.

Many men who are forever talking about women's inhibitions would find it nearly impossible to lie back and let a lover massage them. After about a minute and a half the man sits up and wants to do something too.

Train yourself not to worry so much about doing

something or "getting somewhere" in sex. Spend time with a lover, touching and being touched, enhancing your capacity to take as well as to give. The rule—to try *not* to achieve orgasm—may be invaluable for getting started.

One purpose of this is to develop what Masters and Johnson call "sensate focus," or the ability to enjoy tactile pleasure. But you are also cultivating a more general capacity to go slow and enjoy all aspects of your life.

The third guideline is to *decide all by yourself* whether or not you enjoy making love to someone. This isn't a joke. A great many men ask their friends anxiously, "Do you think she's pretty?" Or a woman will look to other women for reassurance: "Isn't he sexy?"

We don't trust our own feelings the way we should. Even if we're strongly attracted to someone, we distrust the attraction. We imagine that other people know what is good or beautiful when they see it, but we don't. So we ask others to confirm our judgment; we may even accept that judgment in place of our own. How many men respond sexually to fat women but demand thinness in their wives because society prefers slender women?

In the same way, we let other people tell us how—as well as with whom—to make love. Try to ignore outside criteria when it comes to the desirability of a particular sexual act. Discover your own wants.

Gene and Nora, a husband and wife, quarreled often. But their sex life satisfied both of them over most of their twenty years of marriage. Gene would lie on top of Nora, bringing his penis and her clitoris into contact. Both found greater excitement in this than in conventional intercourse, and this was what they did most often.

But then Nora read a book by a psychiatrist saying that sexual intercourse was true happiness and everything else was spurious. Despite her twenty years of experience, she elected to trust this authority. She started rebuking her husband for being a poor lover; she herself felt anxious and confused. Nora never stopped to ask herself how an expert could know better than she the acts that would give her most pleasure. Even if nine out of ten women preferred one sexual act to another, as the tenth, Nora should still have done whatever felt best to her.

She asked me earnestly what she ought to do. And I asked *her*, "How dare you distrust your own feelings? Who can tell better than *you* what you enjoy? Find out what it is and go after it! Don't throw it all away on the recommendation of someone who doesn't even know you."

Never judge your mental health by a sexual preference. It has not been established that healthy people prefer one position in intercourse to another—or prefer intercourse to some other act. Surely in sex we can express our own, our unique desires.

If everyone followed the unwritten conventions of the day, sex would only take place between married people, or at least between those in love. The man would be a few years older than the woman, perhaps with a slightly higher IQ. They'd have sex at the end of the day, when they were almost ready to go to sleep, in the bedroom with the lights off or in dim light. And so on.

And so what? Never regard these conventions as guides to better sex. If anything, they were devised as an *antidote* to good sex, at a time when society feared that people would lose the will or energy to lead productive lives if they enjoyed sex too much.

Times do change. Who knows? The expert who wrote Nora's book might change his mind in twenty years. You had better not let someone else's evaluation of any sexual act determine yours.

HOW TO SEE YOURSELF AS A BETTER LOVER

When sex is marvelous, nearly always you'll like your own body and feel at ease with your lover. But let's say it's a first experience with someone, or sex hasn't been too good for you lately. So you feel all kinds of self-doubt. Is my body attractive? Am I young enough? Will I be suave enough and passionate enough and "good" enough? If you're a man, you may worry about the size of your penis; if a woman, you may think your breasts are too small or too large. You may believe that the way you perform in the next hour will determine the whole course of your relationship with your partner.

In other words, you are frightened. Which makes you liable—unless you recognize the danger—to act on that fear and make it worse.

Certain actions are likely to deepen your self-doubt and prolong it. You're starting out with the feeling that you may not be sexually desirable or adequate. If you try to compensate for this feeling, you'll only intensify it. Don't let yourself. Try to follow these five suggestions when you're with a lover, *especially* if you're feeling anxious.

1. **Never disparage your own body.**
2. **Never apologize for your performance.**
3. **Never brag.**
4. **Never pressure your lover for compliments.** "Was it good?" "Was I good?" Be careful, if you compliment the other person, not to push him or her into complimenting you in return.
5. **Make love, not promises.** Don't say, "Oh, by the way. Next week there's a big party in Southampton, and I'd like you to come." Or, "What a coincidence. I happen to know your boss; maybe I can put in a good word for you."

Doing any of these five things almost always means that you're trying to head off complaints from your lover. You're protesting so much that you're *not* a bad lover that it's impossible for you to believe it. By avoiding these tactics, you can increase your feelings of sexual adequacy. Teach *yourself* that you don't need boasts or apologies, that you won't be disqualified from sex forever if you're not a fantastic lover every time. This will not only help your self-image; it's almost sure to make you sexier to others as well. When you brag or put yourself down, your sexual status drops fast. It's hard for the other person to find you attractive when it's clear that you yourself don't.

Don't worry about your reputation as a lover. If you do, the need to uphold that reputation can put enormous pressure on you. For the most satisfying sex life, try to approach it not as a winner or loser but as a fallible—and still sexy—human being.

SEXUAL FREEDOM

I've said not to boast or disparage your body, but what *should* you do? What's the best way to achieve sexual happiness?

The best way is to give yourself freedom. You already know, whether or not you admit it and act on it, what you want and enjoy in sex. But something is holding you back from expressing those wants freely.

That something is often known as morality. Which isn't surprising, since many of us expect morality to limit our lives. But this doesn't have to be so. Your morality can lift you, liberate you, in many ways.

How? By affirming freedom instead of conventionality. No matter what people say, no act is immoral if it has no victim. And no act is good unless it brings pleasure. You are not forcing a sexual act upon a little child or an idiot. You are doing something for mutual pleasure—something that either partner can stop at will.

Thoughts and feelings are never immoral. And sex is the right place to act out your feelings, your fantasies, as long as the other person is willing. Indicate what you'd like if you're not getting it. Be specific. There is no virtue in leaving your satisfaction to luck; in fact, that may confuse and frustrate your partner. Being more open about your desires can also help to vanquish guilt; the desires aren't secret and shameful any more.

Learn the pleasures of your body by masturbation. Consider everything you discover as wonderful truths. And use these discoveries to guide you and your partner during love-making.

Your freedom can extend even further without harming anyone. Look for the role or the roles that you might enjoy. Who are you in the sexual act? Nothing is ridiculous here. If you're sixty and you want to feel sixteen, there is nothing wrong with that. On the contrary, it's harmful to deny yourself pleasure on the grounds that you ought to be "sensible" or "realistic." That is a shortcut to inhibition—and to dull, unsatisfying sex.

The formula for sexual freedom and creativity is simple enough: Discover what you want to do, and then do more of it. Keep doing and discovering, using pleasure as a guide. You will increase your desire and confidence as long as you act without letting convention or fear inhibit you. And your fantasies will grow more distinct, more vivid as your drive increases.

Give your partner the same kind of freedom. Try to learn the roles he or she wants to play. Don't judge someone's maturity or worth from his fantasies; that can only inhibit your own fantasizing. Instead, strive for an approach to sex in which you are eager to give and receive pleasure in every way you can think of.

Creating sexual freedom depends in part on expanding your freedom in everyday life. We've all seen people mellowed by a good sex life. And we know the effect an unhappy sex life can have on someone's state of mind. But the impact also works the other way. If you're depressed or paranoid until ten-thirty at night, you probably won't be able to put those feelings aside for sex at eleven.

The qualities you cultivate in yourself all day long will influence your sexuality. Everything you do to enhance your daily life—especially your sense of freedom, of enjoyment, of romance, of creativity—will enhance your sexual life as well.

HOW TO BE LIKED 17

We all want to be liked—and loved. We want to know we count to others, to feel important, cherished. And we want to have people we can talk to, people who'll share our joys and disappointments.

The world is full of books and articles that tell us how to get what we want—how to be liked—by making ourselves pleasing to other people. The way to be liked is to make yourself likable. Be agreeable, try not to offend, tell the people what they want to hear. Act sophisticated with the people you meet at work, down-to-earth with the folks back home.

But wait a minute. The Principle says that your actions always reinforce the motive behind those actions. And what's the motive here? Well, it's a kind of fear that you won't be liked for yourself. It's a little bit sheepish, apologetic, as if you were telling the world, "Look, people, I know my true self isn't much, so I'll try to be what you want."

Every time you act on this motive, you make it stronger; you reinforce the fear that, in fact, you don't amount to much. And a curious thing can happen: you can make yourself more popular than you've ever been but end up *feeling all alone.*

It isn't enough to be liked; you also have to *feel* liked —and liked for what you really are. Many self-help books don't acknowledge this. They recommend that you study what other people are looking for—as if it were a commodity—and try to give them that commodity. *Which, as the Principle shows us, is a method that's almost guaranteed to destroy your chances of feeling liked.*

"Books say nice things about you," observes one writer. Therefore, "Line your walls with books." Imagine the young woman for whom that advice is intended. She's being told that the right man will want someone more "intellectual" than she is—that she can only attract him through fraud.

Whether or not this strategy works—whether or not a man likes her better for it—the woman can only like herself less. Through her actions she's taught herself that she isn't really good enough for the kind of man she wants. Even if the man loves her and her book-lined apartment, she has made it impossible to *feel* loved, because she can't know if he's responding to her or to the façade.

It happens all the time. For the sake of going over well with someone, we put on some kind of mask and keep ourselves—our real selves—in hiding. We pretend to be somebody else—chatty or "helpful" or "artistic" or a loyal supporter of the right political party. And so, no matter how well people respond, how can we feel appreciated? We can't. No one knows who we really are. And if we wear masks too much of the time, even we can forget who we really are.

Meantime, if we're constantly working to be liked by everyone we encounter, we reinforce the need for that liking. Which means that after meeting new people we feel an irksome anxiety. Even when we reflect about people we've known for some time we're anxious if we cannot "read" their approval.

Sometimes the strategy backfires in more ways than one. We're trying so hard to be all things to all people that we make ourselves seem insignificant. We lack personal force; we don't impress people. "Oh, him—he's so anxious to please." But even if this doesn't happen, even if our routines go over big, we're reinforcing the worst possible belief about ourselves: the belief that no one would like us the way we are.

I overheard a man at a party saying, "So we had nowhere to go about two last night, and we found ourselves in a little nightclub on the edge of town." I knew the man; he was in his late forties, he had divorced his wife recently, and he was talking to a very attractive woman in her early twenties. Something was out of character for him. I remembered that this man was a nervous, over-scrupulous businessman, who thought six times before he did anything. He never had "nowhere to go," and he never "found himself" anywhere. He was pretending his life was jaunty and loose, because he thought a young woman would require that. Even if she had responded (which she didn't; she could sense he was putting on an act) how could he enjoy a relationship with her? He'd have to keep pretending that he was someone else. Whenever we do this— *package* ourselves in a false wrapping and market the package—we can never be sure that the person wants the real contents.

The way to be liked—the right way—is to cultivate qualities that you can like in yourself. Qualities that seem so worthwhile to you that the people you really want for your friends *ought* to like you for them. Then work on developing these qualities for their own sake, for your own sake, without trying to impress anyone else. In a way, being liked always has to come second, like having an orgasm in sex or becoming famous as a writer or painter. If it's your main goal, you can ruin not only your chances for success but also your capacity for enjoyment.

But what qualities? I'm going to mention eight, observed over years of practice, that may surprise you. They have nothing to do with the assets so many self-help books tell you to cultivate: good looks, charm, status symbols, influential contacts. None of these things is good in itself, unless you know how to handle it. And people will like or dislike you for just that—for the way you handle the assets you have. We've all known people who weren't gorgeous or polished or rich, who had more friends, and closer friends, than other people who were. What did these people have in their favor? Almost certainly they had qualities that allowed them to *like themselves* no matter what their circumstances.

Qualities like the ones I'm going to mention. All of them can make you more likable—to yourself as well as to other people.

1. **Try to learn how to be alone.** This is probably the most surprising—and the most helpful—recommendation I'm going to make.

   But should it be so surprising? Think of it this way: If you can't enjoy your own company, how can you expect others to enjoy it? On the other hand, if you know how to spend time on your own, people will sense this about you—and they'll see it as a strength.

   Millions of people, perhaps most people, suffer from a fear of solitude. Not knowing how the Principle works, they do the worst thing for it: they make sure that they're never alone. "I have to find something to do tonight; Terry isn't going to be home." Every time they rush out to protect themselves against solitude, they let themselves in for a fresh attack of fear. Fear of what? Fear that, as one person put it, "I'm nothing by myself."

   This fear also comes across to other people. Maybe you crowd your friends, just a little; you stay on the phone too long, or invade their privacy sometimes, or insist on seeing them when they're busy. Or perhaps you draw too much attention to yourself in a group, as if you're afraid of being overlooked and abandoned. You may ask for small favors to get people to prove that they really like you. Millions of people do these things. And they always like themselves less for it—and lose stature with other people. The inability to be alone can give you a slightly infantile aspect.

If you can enjoy being alone, you can seek others out of strength, not weakness. You're calling your friends about dinner because you want to see them, not because you can't stand to eat by yourself once in a while. And your friends can feel liked, valued, and not merely depended on. *You become more likable*—to anyone who's open to having a real friend and isn't just seeking someone who's weaker than he is.

Practice being alone. If you're used to spending all your time with people, this will feel as uncomfortable at first as it does to break any habit. While you're feeling uneasy, use the method of magnification to explore your feelings. Why are you constantly hoping the phone will ring? Are you worried about a particular relationship? Do you bore yourself? Try to think of actions you can take— talking to the friend you're concerned about, starting a creative project—to overcome these fears. Then take that action. But don't feel that you have to be doing something "constructive" the whole time to make up for your strange behavior in spending time alone. If you give yourself a chance—perhaps you can start by spending just one or two afternoons a month by yourself—you can learn to enjoy the pleasure of your own company.

2. **Cultivate the ability to see—and enjoy—people as individuals.** It's been said that the art of pleasing is to be pleased. There are very different things to respect and admire in different people. But it's hard to appreciate these things unless you get in the habit of looking for the qualities that make each person unique.

Some of us tend to fit people into categories: "Oh, people under thirty/people over thirty/office workers/factory workers/rich people/men/women are all alike." And we think that only the members of a few of these categories are our kind of people.

There are two problems with this. First, you limit yourself. When you say you only like certain types of people, you're teaching yourself to be a bit nervous around everyone else. And you're probably missing a chance to get to know someone who's marvelously different from the other people you know.

The second problem? When you rely too much on categories, you don't give yourself a chance to respond to people as they really are. Your friends may sense this and resent it; they may even come to feel that your "liking" has little to do with them personally.

A physician I know was distressed when his fiancée said she would only marry a doctor. For years, even before they had met each other, she'd dated only doctors. "She wants to marry a category, not a person," he said to me, and he told her the same thing.

"But becoming a doctor is a real accomplishment," she assured him.

"I know. But I got the degree fifteen years ago. I'd like to feel you were interested in *me*, not just my profession."

It calls to mind Oscar Wilde's young woman who would only marry a man named Ernest; it wasn't very flattering to the young men she knew, whether or not their names qualified.

Don't make your friends feel this way. Practice *not* classifying people, not labeling them as impressive or ordinary or your type or not your type. Talk as little as possible about all the traits you usually use to put people into categories.

For example, a man always mentions the ages of the women he's seeing. He hardly ever talks about a woman without saying how old she is and whether he thinks she's pretty. Every time he does this, he makes youth and prettiness more important to him—which tends to make him feel old. And he's likely to alienate people, both men and women, who don't like the way he tries to turn individuals into types.

Look for what's different, special in every person you meet. Maybe you'll like them and maybe not, but if you do at least you'll be liking them for themselves.

3. **Develop your capacity for pleasure.** A woman once commented to me that she was a good mother. I didn't answer, but I thought about her approach to life. She couldn't plunge into a swimming pool or enjoy the water, even though she went swimming every day. She played tennis every so often, but she didn't much care for it; she played cards with the

same indifference. She didn't enjoy meeting people or seeing new things and places. While she worked hard for her child, she gave the impression that life was grim. In turn, her child loved her but tended to avoid her. If you don't do the things you enjoy in life, you're cheating yourself not only of joy but also of the chance to be likable.

How to enjoy life more? First, slow down; take time to savor the things you do. Get involved as much as you can in the world around you; if you stay on the sidelines, you'll make yourself feel that you aren't very important and neither is what's going on. Keep looking for good experiences—expect them to happen, and celebrate when they do. Try to repeat the experiences, to reinforce the feelings, but don't hang back from new activities and potential pleasures.

4. **Avoid cynicism.** This too will help to preserve your capacity for pleasure. If you're a cynic, you're likely to feel that everyone's out purely for his own gain. No one, you're convinced, is genuine or generous in this world; people only want to get something from others.

A cynic is a difficult friend to have. It's hard to tell a cynic that you've fallen in love or have started a sculpture or are planning to go back to school; the cynic is almost sure to debunk your venture.

Cynicism not only isn't likable; it doesn't help you to like yourself either. Most cynicism starts out as a rationalization for your own failure at some point. Maybe you've become dishonest or have compromised yourself in business or in a marriage. You say that everyone's dishonest, that it's a dog-eat-dog world. Or you say that members of the opposite sex are only out for all they can get.

Worse than the lapse from your own standards is the cynicism you use to cover it up. Every time you sneer at the world in general, you reinforce a belief that people—including yourself—will always turn out to be disappointing. Instead, try to recognize that we all make mistakes and allow yourself to start acting in ways that will reinforce hope.

You can do yourself and your friends a favor by not expressing cynicism; the less you talk about it and act on it, the less you'll feel. And the less you'll inflict it on others, who don't need or want it. As Goethe said, "If you have hope, hurry and give it to me. But if you have doubts, please keep them to yourself. I have enough of my own."

5. **Be ready to confront people when you disagree with them about something that matters to you.** This is important in giving yourself a sense of purpose and identity. And it lets others know that you're capable of strong beliefs and strong feelings. It's hard to like anyone who isn't.

Don't be a tag-along. If you are, you'll reinforce the doubt, "What is there to like about me?" And that doubt will be partly right.

6. **Try to develop empathy—the ability to feel and to care about other people's experiences.** This makes your own life richer, more connected to others' lives. And it makes you more likable.

There are people who can't empathize at all. They commit one faux pas after another without embarrassment, and they're astonished when friends get upset with them. "How was I to know that Shelley would make such a fuss when I told her she ought to lose weight?"

To learn to empathize with other people's feelings, you can start by studying your own experiences. If you remember the way you felt, you can often get an idea of the way someone else might feel in a particular situaion. For instance, you remember your feelings of helplessness when a good friend was ill. Now another friend tells you that his wife is undergoing diagnostic surgery, and he can't stand just having to wait. The better you've understood your own experiences, the better you'll be able to feel for his.

Encourage people to talk about their feelings and their lives if they want to. Do your best to remember what they say, and try to get a sense of what their experiences feel like. The more you do this, the easier and the more natural it'll get for you, and the closer you'll feel to all human beings.

7. **Learn to root for your friends.** "Anyone can sympathize with another's sorrow, but to sympathize with another's joy is the attribute of an angel," wrote Schopenhauer.

Strive for this attribute. What blocks you from rejoicing at people's success? Perhaps envy or some secret fear inhibits you. If so, it makes you less of a friend—and less confident and secure in your own life. When you fail to enjoy a friend's achievements, you are reinforcing some kind of fear, maybe the fear that you're not as "good" as he is or that he'll leave you behind. Parents sometimes damage their relationship with their children by not rejoicing enough in the children's success. Every sign of the child's growing independence is seen as a threat: "I won't be needed anymore. I'm not indispensable."

The more you act on this kind of fear—by withholding praise, or perhaps by subtly disparaging or sabotaging your friend's efforts —the more it can poison your outlook and your friendships. Stop acting on it. Stop reinforcing the fear so that you can learn to enjoy other people's triumphs. It will be a tremendous relief to you as well as your friends.

8. **Finally, remember what the Principle tells you about your life.** It tells you that *you are what you create,* so that you can create the kind of person you want to be. You're the force behind your own life. And other people are the force behind their own lives. You needn't see yourself as a victim or see anyone else that way; you are equals with the power of self creation, a power that deserves respect in yourself and in other people.

You may think of other qualities that you find admirable and wish to cultivate. Whatever they are, look for actions to reinforce them. And make sure that you don't act in these ways only when you're with someone you want to like you.

Maybe the person you want to marry demands punctuality, and you're used to being late. You manage to show up on time when you're meeting this person, but you're still late for everyone else. This means that you are only doing it to impress—not out of conviction—and the action won't give you pleasure or strengthen you. It'll make you a kind of slave to the person you're trying to please.

Very likely you want to become more punctual out

of consideration for others. But do it only because you believe it's truly fair, *which means doing it no matter whom you're going to meet*; otherwise don't do it at all: it would not make you more considerate, only more docile.

To be liked, don't try to please others; try to please yourself—your highest self. Act to uphold and reinforce the values that you believe in, and you'll be able to feel that your friends are liking you for the right things.

Let's say that you place a high value on loyalty to your friends. You've promised to help one friend move, when another, more glamorous friend offers you a weekend trip on his new boat. If you take the trip, even if you have a wonderful time, you're likely to feel that there's not quite as much to like and respect in yourself as you once thought there was. If you turn the trip down, you will respect yourself more, you will feel more likable, and you will feel you have earned that likability.

It isn't enough just to be liked. The *right* way to be liked is by doing only those "attractive" things that are natural and attractive to you yourself. If you don't, you'll never be warmed by others' good feelings about you—and it will hardly matter what they feel.

HOW TO BE RIGHT **18**

The high school was running an art contest for charity. On Sunday afternoon dozens of parents paid five dollars each to drink punch, eat cookies, and see their children's work. At the refreshment table, Laura started talking to Harry, a man she didn't know.

"What do you think of the pictures?" she asked.

"Oh, I don't know anything about art. I just came because my wife wanted to." Looking around, Harry spotted a huge painting with a blue ribbon attached. "That one's supposed to be good, I think."

Laura mentioned that her son had entered the contest and lost. "Oh, I'm sorry," Harry replied at once. "You must be disappointed." Throughout the conversation he was fidgeting and looking uncomfortable. He was obviously thinking, What am I supposed to say to this stranger? Finally he sighted his wife across the room and said quickly, "Well, I've got to go now. My wife wants to leave."

Laura told me about this conversation with disgust. In his efforts not to offend, Harry was more offensive to her than he would have been if he'd said all the work looked like kindergarten stuff. Not only did he refuse to take a stand on any part of the exhibit, he even denied responsibility for coming or going. He was only obeying his wife.

And Laura was bored to death talking to him for even five minutes. People like Harry—afraid to reveal their opinions and desires, often find themselves with virtually nothing to talk about. So they fill in the gaps by talking about what they think other people want to hear. They're reporters, researchers, observers. And sometimes they're presumptuous.

Whether or not he realizes it, Harry's motto is *Don't take a stand*. Ever. Don't commit yourself to any idea or action that isn't thoroughly authorized and endorsed. Why? Because people will laugh at you if you're wrong. Or hate you and feel jealous if you're right. You can't win if you identify yourself with anything.

So Harry thinks. But what is true about paranoia holds true here: You can't win if you *don't* take chances. Every time you efface yourself, say, by remarking that the critics panned a movie rather than remarking that you liked it, you reinforce your belief in the dangers of making your presence felt, and so go through life with a sense of fear and unworthiness. You're not likely to be very interesting to others, either, if every opinion you voice can be found in the local newspaper.

Many people suppress their personalities in smaller ways. For instance, by hiding their own wants behind other people's. "My daughter needs my help over the holidays," Gloria explains, when really she wants to spend the time with her family. The premise is that her own wants don't count; they aren't legitimate. Next time she may lose out on a visit altogether by refusing to admit that she'd like an invitation.

Bill, a mid-level executive, has his own way of keeping his personality down. He's sure he won't get anywhere in his business unless he goes along with everything his superiors say. Which gets tough sometimes, when the superiors disagree with each other. Trying to keep his balance—to please everyone—gets to be more and more of a habit. He starts acting the yes-man at home, at parties, as well as at work. Self creation is taking place: Each act of self-effacement reinforces Bill's conviction that self-effacement is necessary, and that his own judgment is worthless. Gradually he loses touch with his real wants; his life loses vigor and excitement. And it turns out that someone at work with ideas of his own is promoted ahead of him.

Suppressing your individuality can also suppress your appetite for living. And evading responsibility makes you believe you're helpless. You start feeling resigned, fatalistic. There is an ironic effect here: You avoid responsibility, become fatalistic, and this reduces your ability to recognize that you're the cause of what is happening to you—that your own actions create your attitudes. But it's also the precise kind of moment when recognizing this is most vital.

The following ten suggestions can help. Try them for at least a few weeks. In each case you'll be avoiding some act that's motivated by fear of revealing yourself—and so reinforces that fear. Refraining won't be easy if you don't have a clear sense of what you stand for, but later on I'll suggest ways to clarify your own goals.

One of the aims of these exercises is magnification—making your real motivations clear and bringing out the discrepancy between what you think you're doing and what you're actually achieving. So, during these few weeks, try to eliminate distractions: Your goal is to think about your inner life. If you can, stick to a schedule of times to get up, work, eat, sleep. This way the decisions about your external life can be made automatic, non-demanding. Preoccupation with the details of daily life can get in the way of the introspection you're out to promote.

During this trial period:

1. Don't blame anyone or anything else for

your troubles. In fact, don't talk about your troubles at all; or talk of them only in terms of the next step—where you can go from here. Looking for sympathy—trying to make yourself feel better for the moment—actually *weakens* your sense of personal strength. And so does picturing yourself as a pawn or a victim.

2. **Don't attribute your choices to other people.** If *you* fire the babysitter, don't say your wife insisted on it.

3. **Don't quote anyone else's opinions.** You're suggesting a restaurant; don't say that so-and-so recommended it. Take responsibility for the idea. Quoting others might not hurt ordinarily, but if you have a weak sense of self this will make it worse. So don't quote anyone for several weeks, and see what the method of magnification reveals. Do you feel better or not much different—or do you feel lost?

4. **Once you do something, don't deny responsibility for it even if it's a disaster that was actually someone else's idea.**

5. **Avoid the word *we*.** When you turn down an invitation, say that *you're* tired, whether or not it's also true for your mate. Speak in the first person singular.

6. **Don't tell other people how *they* feel.** "I'm sure you don't like this." "I know how John makes you uncomfortable, so I won't invite him." Other people's feelings change, as yours do. You can ask someone how he feels, but don't tell him. Telling him is a particularly anxious version of being a yes-man, trying to anticipate constantly what others will want to hear. The result? Increased fear

of just being yourself—and probably some annoyed friends.

7. **Don't let other people tell you not to feel as you do.** Remind them (gently, if possible) that your feelings of the moment are involuntary—and that you have a right to them no matter what. Never apologize for them just to keep the peace.

8. **When you talk about yourself to friends or strangers—don't give only the facts.** During these weeks give as few facts as possible: substitute opinions and reactions. Avoid status symbols that might impress strangers (who'll then know you as the owner of that yacht and not as Terry Smith). Also avoid fillers, like a detailed account of everything you did that day from six A.M on.

9. **Don't *get* only the facts.** When you meet people, avoid asking for the census information: where they were born, went to school, work, live. Try to get to know them as individuals without this information. This will be difficult, but it's a step toward breaking the cycle of fear—fear that you'll reveal something about yourself, constantly reinforced by avoiding real conversations.

10. **Don't rehearse anything you say in this period.** Don't tell a story if you know just how it'll come out. Memorized accounts reinforce the fear of saying the wrong thing if you're spontaneous.

In all likelihood you'll feel uncomfortable during these few weeks. You've spent years suppressing your identity and ideas, and now you're doing just the opposite: You're asserting yourself, talking positively, acting on the belief that you are justified in having opinions, and that they are worthy of respect. Remember this: the discomfort will subside as you go on reinforcing the new premise and *it* begins to feel natural. Your new sense of entitlement will become less occasional, more a steady thing in your life. This won't happen overnight, among other reasons because there is probably a cluster of other tactics suppressing your identity, which you don't yet recognize as harmful. But your job will be to discover this set of tactics that downgrade you and to root them out. You won't be able to identify or stop every single harmful tactic from day one; just make a start. After these first few weeks it'll become easier.

At the same time, here are some more positive things to do:

1. **When someone asks you how you feel about something, answer** *as quickly as possible*. Don't censor your response. You have the right to any reaction you feel—even if you feel like strangling someone. Saying you'd like to kill someone doesn't commit you to doing it; you might simply decide not to play cards with the person tomorrow. A quick answer is nearly always more authentic than a slow one—and you're trying to break the habit of avoiding true responses.

2. **Before you make** *any* **phone call, write down your purpose in making it.** You may want to ask a question, negotiate something, or hear the voice of a friend. Come to the point quickly, and try not to stay on the phone much longer. The purpose of this exercise is to sharpen your awareness of the way you pursue your goals through everyday actions. I'm not saying this crispness of purpose is necessary for everyone all the time; but it does relieve the problem discussed in this

157

chapter. In particular, notice during the call any welling impulse to say or elicit something that's obviously beyond the written purpose for the call. Ask yourself: "Was I really trying to fool myself by writing down a nice, respectable, 'healthy' reason for the call when the real motivation was something else?" It's essential to be able to identify your true motivations because it's *they* that are going to be reinforced by what you do. No one is forcing you to make the call—you're *choosing* to make it to carry out your purpose. And sometimes the honest articulation of the purpose will show you it's a call you shouldn't make at all.

For example, your cover story to yourself for calling Jim—the alleged impulse behind reaching for the phone—is to remind him of a meeting coming up; but on honest reflection you know the real reason is to hear him reassure you about something. Don't reach for reassurance.

3. **Keep this phrase in mind: *No one's forcing you.*** Don't describe anyone—including yourself—as a victim of circumstances. Sally can't stand her job or her marriage, but she doesn't *have* to stay in either. Dave didn't *have* to make snide comments about his rival in front of the boss. There are very, very few things you'll ever be forced to say or do. You can start recognizing this by looking for ways other people *choose* to do what they do and aren't forced into it.

4. **Talk about the *present* instead of the past.** Try—for as long as it takes to feel comfortable with it—not mentioning anything that happened more than a day ago. This focuses

your attention on your daily decisions and feelings.

5. **Answer the following questions:**

- What are your chief goals?
- What do you love?
- When—in what situations—are you most likely to show courage?
- When are you *least* likely to show it?
- How do you work at getting what you want?
- You're ninety-five and dying. You're lamenting your failure to have acted a certain way. What is it?
- You're ninety-five and regretting you never had certain experiences. What are they?
- What four potentially true sentences would you most like mankind to write on your tombstone?
- What four potentially true sentences would you *least* like written there?
- What people do you hate?
- If you were on a life raft in a raging ocean and could save six people among everyone you know, who would they be and why?

You don't have to answer these questions for all time. Since you choose what's important to you, you can choose to change it. Once you recognize that you do want things—and what those things are—you can start going after the goals you continue to believe in and revise the ones you don't.

6. **Keep an "emotional diary" for a few months or longer if it continues to help you.** Write down two events that occur each day. Describe in some detail the decisions you make

and your reactions. Look for and record various kinds of emotions—don't limit yourself to recording discomfort, such as embarrassment or envy or outrage at the way you've been treated. Note also when you feel proud, confident, exultant, sympathetic.

After a while, you'll be able to see what leads to these kinds of feelings. You always feel clumsy or unimportant after you see Barry and Sue. Or you tend to feel terrific around Jules and Allison. What choices did *you* make that contributed to this result? For instance, you chose to be silent when Barry and Sue told jokes against friends of yours. You like the way you expressed yourself to Jules and Allison, who pay close attention when you talk about yourself.

You'll sharpen your sense of control over your own life as you keep this diary. And as you examine the circumstances that go along with these feelings, you'll arrive at useful insights about your own behavior.

You can start being right instead of wrong or wronged all the time. You can be the chooser, the mover, the molder of your own life. Instead of seeing yourself as a broken figure crushed by the odds against you, you can be a romantic hero fighting against those odds. *And winning.*

HOW TO MAKE UP YOUR MIND 19

What happens when you have to make a decision? Any decision: a simple one like what to wear today or where to eat lunch. Or a more complicated one: Should I go to law school, quit my job, move in with my lover, buy that baseball team? Can you make up your mind and get on with it, or do you worry excessively about the consequences?

And if you worry, are you sure you know what you're worrying about? Marjorie, a widow of thirty-six, told me that she spent weeks deciding where to put a picture of her dead husband. First it would go to the attic, then back to her bedside table. Then up to the attic again—and so on.

Finally, her six-year-old son said to his sister, "Mommy doesn't know what to do with Daddy." And he was right. For two years Marjorie had been going out with Joel, a local businessman, and now he wanted to marry her. But she couldn't decide where to put her first husband—in other words, whether to start a new life with another man. Once she realized what the issue was, it didn't matter where she put the picture. More important, she was able to concentrate on the real decision: to marry or not to marry. Two weeks later she put the picture away for good and accepted Joel's proposal.

Indecision about one thing is often a sign of conflict about something else. Frank couldn't decide whether to buy a plaid or a solid gray suit. The plaid seemed too loud, the gray too conservative. Whenever he went back to the store (and the salesmen were getting used to seeing him almost every lunch hour) determined to buy, say, the plaid suit, he started wondering if the gray wasn't more appropriate.

At the time Frank was trying to learn to be more assertive. He'd spent most of his childhood with a very strict uncle who believed that young people had to learn to "behave"—or else. And this uncle bought him only old-fashioned, uncomfortable clothes that had to be kept clean at all costs.

Frank grew up behaving—all too well. He was shy and afraid to advance his own ideas. Twice he lost promotions: No initiative, they said.

It wasn't really two suits Frank was trying to decide between; it was two ways of life. And he was afraid to choose either one: to keep his conservative life, which hadn't brought him much joy or success, or to take a chance and risk making a fool of himself. Even a small risk, like wearing a plaid suit, frightened him; he could hear it now—"Look at that mousy guy in the flashy clothes."

Frank's fears—fear of self-assertion and fear of criticism and fear of change—make him indecisive. (And in turn indecisiveness aggravates his fears.) Nearly always, when you or I can't make decisions, some kind of fear is the reason.

Fear of ridicule, for instance, can keep us debating the pros and cons of the simplest issue for hours. Do I have the nerve to buy that red satin bedspread? Should I ask Ed to go out for a drink after work? Should I serve steak or stuffed eggplant when the Bradleys come for dinner? Let's see, they might sneer at steak—it's not exactly creative—but at least they can't say I'm cheap. And the eggplant might not come out right. On the other hand. . . .

And then there's the fear of being *categorized*. This is almost a kind of claustrophobia; you believe that choosing to do one thing means that you can't do anything else. That you'll be boxed in and labeled for life. This is a very common mind-set: Athletes can't also be thinkers; you can only be good in English or math, not both; you can't like classical *and* rock music.

Very bright, talented people often suffer from this claustrophobia. Blake, an actor who badly needed money, was afraid that driving a cab several hours a day would dissipate his talent. And there was a brilliant young woman who couldn't decide between medicine and singing—and so took a menial job while she tried to decide. And stayed there for five years; she *still* couldn't decide. Eventually she went on to medical school, but in those five years, which were lost to indecision, she could have done a lot more with both pursuits.

Fear, regret, and inefficiency all go along with the inability to make up your mind. You waste time and energy deciding what to do, and then you waste *more* time wondering if you should have done something else. You're likely to lose your sense of humor—after all, you have so many weighty decisions on your mind. You grow very dependent on other people's advice and opinions. And in the end, it may seem to you that the world is hostile, just waiting to pounce on your first wrong move.

As usual, there's a cycle of habits here that you have to break. Start by practicing a "high speed drill" whenever you're faced with a small decision. If you need, for instance, to choose a movie, write a letter, or buy a coat, set a time limit. For the movie it might be something like five minutes; for the letter, one hour; for the coat, two or three hours.

Force yourself to make a decision in the given time,

and then stick to it. (Don't write a letter and tear it up, or take the coat back to the store the next day.) You can expect to feel that you're making disastrous, irresponsible choices; that feeling is what the problem's all about. But a few days later you'll probably find that you're much more satisfied with your choices than you thought you'd be.

Of course, you shouldn't use this drill for major, lasting decisions. Don't decide to get married or divorced, have a baby, or invest thousands of dollars in a strict time limit of minutes or hours. But the drills should give you more confidence in your ability to decide such issues when they come up.

Many artists use similar drills to give themselves the freedom to experiment and make mistakes. They do sketches in three minutes flat, or perhaps without lifting the pencil from the paper. If the picture is wonderful, fine; if not, it has helped them to overcome perfectionism. Trying to be perfect all the time is the best way to get nothing done. It's like putting off a letter until you can think of exactly the right words: What if you never do?

Besides, the Principle is always at work. The longer and harder you think about a decision, the more crucial it seems to you. Even if it's about something trivial.

The five exercises below, along with the speed drills, can help you get rid of the feeling that it's not safe to trust your own judgment.

1. **Stop apologizing for every mistake.** This is a form of indecision: You do your best at something and then attack yourself as if your efforts were worthless. And every time you make an unwarranted apology you strengthen the idea that you are a grievous offender in life. Uncomfortable as it may be at first, *not* apologizing will start you thinking—and keep

reinforcing the thought—that mistakes are allowed.

2. **Defend other people's right to make mistakes.** Be especially careful not to scapegoat anyone for mistakes or impropriety when you yourself are nervous.

Wilma, who was lonely in a new city, had a bad word for everyone who went to singles bars. They were tramps, she said, absolutely desperate. When one of the women in her office invited her to go along with a group to a new bar, she was torn: she actually wanted to go—but how could she after condemning the very idea? She could just imagine people using her own words against her.

The more contributions you make to a tolerant world, on the other hand, the more you'll believe that the world is a tolerant place.

3. **Don't glorify the past or describe the present as inferior.** People who are indecisive often idealize others who *seemed* perfect when they were young. They're still struggling to live up to these perfect standards (more about this later), and so worry more about imperfections.

Instead of assuming that anyone you once admired was perfect, assume that (among other things) he was *decisive*—and so no one took much notice of his mistakes. Aim for decisiveness, not perfection.

4. **Stop asking people for advice.** If you're indecisive, you probably have a group of experts you look to for suggestions. Next time you have to buy something, especially anything that has to do with your image, like clothes

or furnishings for your house, don't ask anyone about it, not your mother or brother-in-
law or neighbor with such good taste. Make
your own mistakes.

5. **Don't copy other people.** If you always take
your vacations where your sister takes hers,
go somewhere else. If that neighbor with the
good taste has one kind of car, don't buy the
same kind. Once again, make your own mistakes. Or perhaps you'll find that your own
ideas are better. More important is the self
creation principle at work: By acting on the
belief that you *can* have good original ideas,
that you *can* make your own decisions, you
strengthen that belief in yourself.

As you follow these suggestions, you'll go through the
usual stages of breaking a habit. You'll feel very anxious
at first, then more comfortable. This doesn't mean you'll
always know what to do at the end of it all—you'll still
have mixed feelings at times—but you'll be able to go
ahead and *act* in spite of those mixed feelings. Whereas,
when you started out, you had the same mixed feelings—
or worse—and took forever to get things done.

In the beginning, when you're most anxious about
making the wrong choices, see what you can learn about
yourself. Use the method of magnification: Ask yourself
what's the worst that can happen. That your parents will
get furious? That you'll start running wild? That you'll
be laughed at? That you'll lose your friends or your job?

Some of these fears—like Marjorie's fears of betraying
her deceased husband—just won't survive the light of day.
They'll disappear when you look hard at them. Others can
be more persistent, like Frank's fear of asserting himself.

If you find secret fears behind your indecisiveness,
think hard about them. Do they seem realistic? Why are

they so important? Maybe someone will laugh at you. But would that be so bad?

Remember that no one act can determine your whole life: Frank could buy the plaid suit but then make decisions like his earlier ones, if he wanted to. There are ways and ways of wearing a suit, after all; if he wears it and slouches more than ever, as if atoning for his one daring decision, it won't change his life at all. But if he *wants* to start a new pattern and takes other steps to continue it, he can build on the single decision. His next move might be speaking up at a business meeting. Or asking that interesting co-worker out for lunch.

If you're secretly afraid of being categorized, simple scheduling might do wonders. Most people can pursue several ambitions, over a lifetime if not simultaneously. Depending on what you want to do—be a pilot, a CPA, a parent; learn Sanskrit; build a ski lodge; travel around the world, whatever—you can probably work out a schedule that allots certain hours to certain ventures, or it may have to be certain years.

Finally, as you scrutinize your fears, you might find that certain people seem to "make" you afraid. You love to give parties, but when the Harrises are coming you take twice as long to decide what wine, what cheese, even what crackers to serve. (Or maybe you'd better bake some fresh bread. They always seems to have it at their house.) Or you worry much more than usual about your clothes when you plan to get together with Lee and Norman.

Ask yourself why you're so worried about pleasing these people. Are they hypercrictical? And if so, how do you deal with their criticism? If not, try to think if you want something special from them and so feel unnaturally dependent. There's trouble in any relationship if it makes you indecisive; the best friendships are the ones in which you feel the most freedom to make errors.

Try assuming that this freedom exists. Give yourself

a time span, such as a morning, to shop for the party, and stick to it. By doing this, you give the people who are coming the benefit of the doubt, in assuming that they will appreciate what you've prepared. Treat their criticism (if there is any) like any other—worth listening to but not worth hating yourself for.

Indecisiveness usually develops out of relationships with highly critical adults, especially parents. You hesitate because you get the feeling your parents will be right there, calling you stupid if you make the wrong choice. And you may find that the specific people who make you nervous are fulfilling your parents' old role in your life.

Try to imagine exactly what the Harrises will say if they don't like your wine. Then think back to what your parents used to say when *they* didn't like something. If the two are similar (or you get the same sinking feeling when you think about either one), you're giving the Harrises unnecessary power (which they may not want or even know they have) to hurt you. After all, they're not your parents, and by now even your parents shouldn't have all that much power to make you unhappy.

"Do I dare disturb the universe?" wondered J. Alfred Prufrock in a poem by T. S. Eliot.

Dare. You've got much less to lose, and more to gain, than you think.

HOW TO 20 SUCCEED

This isn't a chapter (necessarily) on how to become a millionaire—and it's certainly not about ninety-nine ways to intimidate people. Or about the right clothes to wear to become an executive.

It *is* about any kind of success you want, yet are keeping yourself from. Maybe you long to be a giant of industry, or maybe you'd simply like to play terrific bridge. And there may be no reason why you can't, except that you keep holding yourself back.

I once asked Althea Gibson, the great tennis player, which stroke was hardest for her to hit. I expected her to say something like "cross-court backhand" or "overhead smash." Instead she answered, "The last shot of the match." And went on to explain she was happiest on the court. She didn't want to get off, even as a winner.

Unlike most tennis stars, Gibson went home from the court to a poor, dangerous neighborhood. She was the first black champion in the sport. For her the end of a game meant leaving the plush Forest Hills stadium, the cameras, and the crowds—and going back to a ghetto and friends who could live for several days on the money a tennis fan paid for a ticket.

Not that Althea Gibson let this stop her. She didn't

allow the impulse to stay on the court to inhibit the final smash that made her a champion. But the temptation was always there—and it could be there for you in the same way. And maybe there's more you could do to resist it.

"But what's he talking about? Everyone *wants* to succeed."

Well, yes and no. Many of us want to succeed—but also want not to. We're inhibited about success. Along with our obvious wish to make good is a secret wish to sabotage the whole thing. Somehow there's a hidden reward in failure.

We can be inhibited about a kind of success other people take for granted—like speaking, which somehow turns into stuttering. Or learning to dance. Or driving a car. Or we can be afraid to aim too high. I'm good, but was I really good enough to start my own business? Should I have dared? Somehow it doesn't seem to be working out too well. . . .

Of course, lack of success at something doesn't always mean that you're inhibited. Most people who don't win the U.S. Open Tennis Championship can't blame it on a secret desire to fail. It *is* possible to set unrealistic goals. But here are six signs that can tell you the problem is *inhibition*.

1. Repeated avoidance of a desired activity. You want to ask Robin out but keep backing down at the last minute. Then you hate yourself for being a coward.
2. Extreme self-consciousness. You're always watching yourself like an outside observer. Evaluating. Did I do better or worse last time? How well do most people my age do? What do Lou, Jane, Christopher (etc.) think of me?
3. The feeling that you're unlucky. Circumstances keep thwarting you. You plan to show

guests your pottery one night, but there just doesn't seem to be any break in the conversation. Or it gets very cold on the night you were planning to go to a party, and you've got nothing to wear. The fates are always against you.

4. Overconcern about the environment. You want to do a painting, but first you have to wait until the room's been fixed up, you've found the right clothes, and the light is perfect. But maybe this isn't the right time of day to start. You keep making small adjustments to the environment and never seem to get very much done.

5. A sense that your body keeps getting in the way. Just as someone asks you to sing in public you start to feel dizzy or have to go to the bathroom. You're willing, of course, but your body seems to feel otherwise. You get suddenly sick or exhausted—or may even feel almost paralyzed.

6. Feelings of unreality. As you begin to speak to an audience, you get the sense that it's someone else talking. *You* didn't just tell that joke. This is known as *dissociation*: You're unwilling to be associated with your own act.

After reading this far in this book, you probably know what I'm going to say next. *Go through with it.* Don't give up on whatever you're trying to do—especially if you're convinced that you're botching it. Giving up reinforces a sense of incompetence; going on gives you a commitment to success.

Keep painting even if the light isn't perfect. Speak even if you stutter and someone seems to be looking down on you. You can't help all the self-critical thoughts that may come to mind—at least not until you stop acting on them. And whether or not to act is always in your full control.

Don't indulge your fearful thoughts. Bring out your pottery as planned even if you now feel it's inappropriate. Go to the party. It's much better to perform badly, even to be rejected, than to reject the image of yourself as someone capable of success.

And don't disparage your own performance. Inhibited people are likely to think that others are laughing at them. Often they laugh at themselves before anyone else can—hoping to appease potential antagonists. In other words, inhibited people tend to be slightly paranoid.

Don't indulge (and intensify) such paranoia by belittling yourself. You won't make friends; in fact you're more likely to alienate people. (Why should I think well of Josh when he thinks so badly of himself? After all, he should know.) All of which reinforces your sense of unworthiness for any kind of success.

As you try to succeed, it may help to recognize possible motives for *not* trying. Here are the five most common that I have observed, along with specific ideas for overcoming them:

1. *Fear of arousing envy.* Without realizing it, you associate success with *greed*. You're afraid to be seen trying to surpass your friends or relatives; they'll ridicule you as pretentious and try to bring you down. How dare you go to college when your brothers didn't? Many people with this fear have grown up in highly competitive households; they tend to see all adults—even close friends—as rivals.

   If you feel this way, you probably also feel that people will—and ought to—hate you for trying to outdo them. You're inclined to be secretive about your ambitions and achievements. Compliments make you uncomfortable; it's as if the person giving them had caught you doing something wrong. So you tend to deny you've achieved much of anything: It was easy, you say; I was just lucky. How can people get mad at you if it was all fate?

There are both men and women who are inhibited about buying beautiful clothes. They're afraid others will hate them for trying to look good. If the woman does buy a particularly nice dress, she might pretend it's nothing special ("Oh, this was on sale; it's not real silk") or even sabotage the effect by wearing it with sloppy hair and old shoes.

The cure? Stop pretending you have no aspirations. Let the world know what you want. Thank people if they praise you, no matter how uncomfortable it makes you feel. You would like to excel, make money, have more friends. Admit it. Tell a few people. The opposite—hiding your ambitions—can only make you feel that you shouldn't succeed. So you see that you don't.

It's regrettable that others may be less successful than you. But stunting yourself won't do them any good. Just as pursuing your own goals—assuming you don't start cutting throats—won't do them any harm.

If your "symptoms" include poor posture, speaking in a low voice, and excessive modesty about your achievements, it will help to talk up. At first, you'll feel like a bit of a braggart. But be honest, and if your fears come true and certain people do resent your successes, you might as well face that now.

Hard as it is to acknowledge bitterness from people you care about, it can't do you the harm that self-sabotage does.

Let others show their true colors. If you wish, ask people who resent you just how your achievements will hurt them. (Then *listen* to their answers, and perhaps take another look at Chapter 13, on criticism. Your friends can warn you if you're getting ruthless or overbearing.) If they're simply envious, you might want to chide them for not wishing you well. Remember—and remind your friends—that your being miserable or unsuccessful doesn't make you a better friend to anyone. (Misery may love company, but it just keeps getting more miserable.) In fact, you can do a lot more to encourage others if you've had a success or two of your own.

2. *Fear of ultimate failure.* Another common motive for sabotaging yourself is fear that success will bring demands on you that you can't handle. Valerie says she wants to get married, but she always freezes around eligible bachelors. Meanwhile, married men (and others clearly ineligible) bring out her confidence and charm. She has affairs that can't possibly lead to marriage. Her friends say she really doesn't want to get married. Which is partly true, partly false. She's inhibited because she's not sure she would make an adequate wife.

Valerie isn't afraid of men, she's afraid of marriage. But her fear is cutting her off from both. As a start, I suggested she make a vow not to consider marriage, no matter how well a relationship is going, for at least a year. This will take the pressure off; she can have a marvelous time without worrying about the consequences. And while she's enjoying herself she can work on the real problem: rooting out the actions that are sustaining her fear of proving inadequate as a wife.

Fear of ultimate failure is almost a fear of succeeding too well—of going so far you overreach yourself. We fear the great height because we don't believe we can stay up there, and the fall back down will be too painful, too humiliating. Plan for one success at a time instead of anticipating where it will all lead. Remember that you can always stop at any point—if you should. But in fact if you believe you have any ability at all, and if you let that belief move you to try to achieve something, the very effort will strengthen the belief, your confidence will grow, and, because confidence itself is an asset, your chances of achievement will increase. And as you do strive and achieve, your fear of the great height will diminish. Regard your fear of it as an illusion of childhood, like the little boy's impression that his father is gigantic. When you're that size yourself it will seem only natural.

3. *Fear of independence.* You think no one will care about you unless you're helpless or in trouble. They must have such reasons for paying attention to you, or you'll be lost, overlooked.

There can be some truth to this. Some people find their parents sympathetic only when they're sick or in some kind of crisis. When they're on their feet, their parents disappear. This is painful, but the alternative is more painful. Ultimately, the way other people treat you is less of a problem—does less to your self-esteem—then the way you treat yourself. The self creation principle says that if you act on the premise that your only attraction is as an invalid you'll promote fear of accomplishment—and stunt your life.

Even though success can mean some loneliness, if you're hiding your strengths and hopes from the people close to you, right now you're more alone than you will be if you step forward. Look for people who think of you as strong, who don't cherish you for the weaknesses that make *them* feel strong. As you become more confident, certain people may abandon you, but others will be more attracted. You'll have the chance to become part of a new and different kind of community—made up of individuals who come together for friendship and not mutual protection.

4. *Fear of losing your identity*. It seems that you won't be the same person if you succeed. Somehow learning to dance or shoot pool or write poetry or whatever will undermine everything you stand for.

Sexual stereotypes often contribute to these beliefs. Many men grow up thinking it's unmanly to have strong emotions—except, perhaps, jealousy or a lust for revenge. And many women are taught not to use their minds or they'll be considered cold, threatening, unfeminine. All kinds of inefficiency result. The men aren't as loving or creative as they might be; the women often shy away from science or business or anything that's supposed to be male.

To get rid of this fear, recognize that no ability is incompatible with any other ability. Excellence of one kind *never* implies incompetence of another kind. Especially when it comes to your intellectual and emotional lives —the two can only enhance each other.

5. *Fear of losing your goals.* If you succeed, then what's left? What will be your purpose in life? Some people constantly deny themselves things and experiences in order to save money, but somehow don't save it. But what would they do for incentive if they had money? Others spend all their time and effort trying to lose weight, but don't get thin. What would they live for if they did? The prospect of success is terrifying in this set-up.

Diversifying your goals can ease this fear. Don't only try to lose weight; also try to learn something you always wanted to know. Or set up a schedule: Save money for one purpose; then, after you've spent it on what you wanted start saving for something else.

Every successful life requires an endless sequence of challenges. There is always unfinished business. Whenever you run out of obvious purposes, make it your goal to set a goal. If you have nothing to strive for, you don't strive, and if you don't strive, the self creation principle says that the general sense of possibilities in life, of promise, will wither.

Along with any of these five specific motives for failure, the fear of looking foolish may trouble you. And since you have doubts that you're doing the right thing, you might not have the perspective to ignore unfair critics. The thing to do is to work on those doubts in the ways I've suggested. As you become surer of your right to change, you'll be less vulnerable to other people's reactions.

Sam, a thirty-five-year-old man who spoke somewhat illiterate Brooklyn English, was promised a good promotion if he could improve his speech. He decided to try—and spent hours alone in his room talking back to a tape recorder. Unpleasant thoughts ran through his head: embarrassment, the sense that he was betraying his old friends, loss of identity. He felt he had no right to fancy speech patterns; they were suitable for other people, but not for him. And he wondered if he was giving up the best part of himself—what he saw as a rough, lovable James Cagney image—to become false and pretentious.

A few friends actually did make things harder. They said he'd never talk any differently and was phony for trying. This fitted right in with his own fears and sense of strangeness. Not until he forced himself to continue his efforts—and the new speech became a new habit—did he realize that his friends had underestimated him. And that flawed speech wasn't necessary to his identity. He was still the same person, but with new possibilities open to him.

And that's the point of this chapter—that success is something to pursue and not to fear. Once it becomes a habit, you can only like yourself better for it.

GENEROSITY— OR BRIBERY? 21

Picture this, an everyday scene on city streets:

A grimy man in torn clothes steps out of the shadows and thrusts his hand out at passersby. "Any spare change?" he asks. "You got a quarter?"

Three different men, all reasonably successful, give the man money—but in three different ways. Al says, "Sure," and produces twenty-five cents. Noting that the beggar isn't bad-looking underneath it all, he imagines a history of terrible bad luck. And remembers how worried he's been about his own job. He could lose it and be penniless like this man. For Al the quarter is a cheap insurance payment. Taking care of beggars now will somehow protect *him* if his luck should turn bad. Almost as if there were a federation of beggars that would reward his past generosity.

Nick is terrified when he sees the beggar coming. He's near-sighted and thinks too much about muggings. The combination makes him startle easily. He thinks of running away but stops to hear the beggar. Then, with a thought very like, *he'll kill me if I don't give*, he drops a quarter into the beggar's hand and looks in his eyes for permission to leave. He's astonished when the beggar thanks him and moves away; he walks on slowly, hiding his relief at having paid his way to safety.

The third donor is Paul, a man who's just had a particularly good day. He has always enjoyed giving things to people, and he gladly hands the man a half-dollar. Without pausing to study the beggar's face, he hurries on, thinking about his promotion at work and his plans for changing the office around.

Are these men truly generous? Not all three.

Al and Nick aren't; they're only out to protect themselves. Al is afraid he'll be poor himself someday. Nick imagines that the beggar will attack him if he doesn't pay up. (Nick's convinced he is dealing with potential violence at every turn.) Only Paul, who wants nothing for himself, acts generously. He doesn't expect anything—from the beggar or from the universe—in return. If the act makes him feel good, fine, but he has no ulterior motive.

Does it matter? So Al and Nick may not be generous; still, they're both helping someone out. What's the difference?

The difference is that Al and Nick both *hurt* someone—themselves. They trigger a predictable effect; by acting on fear they make the fear worse. Al renews his terror of losing his money through incompetence on the job. And Nick reinforces his belief that danger lurks on every street corner.

Of course, both Nick and Al feel a temporary sense of relief after leaving the beggar. And they have a nice label for what they've done: It's an act of charity. Of philanthropy. Like most of us, they'd rather see themselves as benefactors than cowards.

But they *are* cowards and staying the same every day. Especially every day that they make a virtue out of renewing their fears.

Many of us do the same thing. We make fearful decisions routinely, paying for protection in various ways. And all the while we tell ourselves how generous we're being. How devoted or kind or thoughtful. We can stay in fear for a lifetime this way.

For instance, millions of parents make unreasonable sacrifices for their children because they're afraid not to. They think, if I don't get little Joey expensive trains or send Laurie to Europe or babysit for the grandchildren whenever I'm asked, my children will think I don't love them. Or worse, they'll decide that they don't love me.

There are husbands and wives desperately eager to please their mates, because they're sure those mates will leave them the minute they don't. Stephanie, for example, who cooked elaborate dinners every night after working all day and always told her husband she didn't need a bit of help around the house, was sure this was what was demanded of a good wife.

Fear-motivated benefactors usually tell themselves: "I'm always happy to help out"; "I want to be useful"; "I'm so glad you liked it; I'll stop by tomorrow to see if there's anything else I can do." But they aren't really enjoying these generous acts; they're constantly filled with anxiety to see how the acts are received. Whether they're being appreciated. Whether they've done enough. And somehow they've *never* done enough to be able to relax their vigilance.

Sometimes apparently generous acts are symbolic. A mother rushes across town to buy the toy her child admired in a window because she can't stand to see the child cry. But her real motive is guilt. She has an affair going on and is away from the child unnecessarily. Buying the toy is a gesture to ease her own conscience (which doesn't work, because it reinforces the idea that she needs to atone for her sins). Not a generous gift to her child.

For some people it's not an act here or there that is motivated by fear, but a whole way of leading their lives. One they pride themselves on. Jay, for instance, thinks he is a kind, good man because he never raises his voice and always tries to stop arguments that are getting heated.

Actually, Jay's fear of disputes dates back to his childhood. When his parents quarreled, he knew they'd soon start screaming and breaking things and disturbing the neighbors. He felt torn between his mother and father and would tremble for days after one of these fights.

When Jay now tries to stay kindly and calm at all times, he's re-creating the world of his childhood. Which constantly reinforces his morbid fear of disruption (which has grown worse with the years, even though there's been less and less to fear).

What passes as kindness need not have any kindness in it. In all these examples, what separates kindness from self-destruction is simple: the motive. An act with a generous motive exhilarates you and makes you feel close to the recipients. While an act based on fear hurts your self-confidence. And isolates you from the very people you're trying to please.

The same act can have different motives at different times. One day you take a friend out for dinner because it's payday and he looks as if he could use cheering up; another day, because you're afraid your friends are losing interest in you. And then there's sex. Sometimes you initiate it or take part because you *want* to—other times, as a way of appeasing your mate.

Or you can start something with one motive and continue it with another. Guy de Maupassant wrote a story about a married woman who meets her lover on Wednesdays for many years. At first she is thrilled by all the preparations: getting her clothes ready, seeing to the carriage, entering her lover's house, hiding his gifts, keeping the whole affair secret. But years later she's going through these motions without any pleasure. She doesn't love the man now; she just wants reassurance that she's still desirable. In the beginning the affair made her feel young. Now it only reinforces her fear of growing old.

So you can't simply look at your acts to see if you're

doing yourself harm; you have to find the *motive*. As always, there are questions to ask yourself if you're uncomfortable after you've done something for someone else. And *before* you start doing any more favors.

The next time you do a "good deed," think about these three questions:

1. *Did your deed give you pleasure, whether or not the other person thanked you enthusiastically (assuming that he or she didn't absolutely attack you for it)?* If so, your motive was a generous wish to give. But if not, you acted in the hopes of getting something in return—probably reassurance. Which only makes you more anxious.

2. *Do you feel closer to the person as a result of your act?* The answer will be Yes if the act sprang from a generous impulse to enhance the person's life. And No if your good deeds were motivated by fear of rejection.

3. *Do you feel stronger or weaker afterward—both immediately and after a few hours or a few days?* Nick, the man who was terrified of the beggar, was overjoyed *at first* that he had bought good will, but later felt more anxious than ever. True generosity makes you feel strong; after all, you have enough—whether it's time or money or talent or love—to share some with other people. Even people who've been through great misfortune have found this to be true; they've gained new strength and hope by acting generously. But acts motivated only by fear make you more fearful.

Once you've seen how you feel after a number of generous acts, try the method of magnification. Stop doing things for others for a specified period of time, say, three weeks or a month. Help *yourself* during this period—not anyone else.

Then study the thoughts that come to mind. If you've been acting out of fear, your thoughts will be extremely anxious. Let's say you always let Gary borrow your car on Sundays, even though there are times you could use it yourself. Stopping will probably make you feel you're letting him down, that he might very well (and not unreasonably) turn against you. But it's still important for you to stop. The fears will get worse the first few times you refuse, but then they'll subside and you'll be free of a whole destructive cycle.

Another example, Buddy. Buddy usually brings his wife flowers after work on Fridays. He thinks he's being loving and thoughtful. But when he stops, he expects her to turn against him, perhaps even to split up with him. The first Friday night without flowers is torture for him. But learning that she still loves him—and even coming to realize that there would be something very wrong if she didn't—is more than worth the initial anxiety. From now on if he brings her flowers it will be an honest expression of love—not a manifestation of fear.

When you stop doing favors, you'll probably get new perspective on ways you've been acting for years. Acts that seemed generous at the time—and certainly harmless— may turn out to be ploys to keep from losing a friend's good will (which may or may not have been in danger). Madeline's down on her luck and keeps asking you for small loans. Which she doesn't repay. There's no doubt that she can use the money, and you haven't wanted to press her to pay it back. Still, you realize you haven't been helping out because you genuinely wanted to, but because you believed that you couldn't refuse. That's the danger sign, the sense that you really don't have a choice.

Have you tended to defend people like Madeline as misunderstood victims? For instance, no one but you seems to see why she couldn't work in a job "beneath" her. If you've got all kinds of excuses for Madeline—or for anyone else who keeps getting your help—you're probably not facing up to the truth: that you're being bullied.

Or take Jay, the peacemaker. When people start fighting, he does everything he can to stop them. He thinks of this as a favor, but also as something necessary. He *has* to stop them or . . . or what? The only thing that can teach Jay his intervention isn't absolutely crucial is stopping to see what happens. When he tries it, he's at first terrified of the consequences. His wife and son are arguing; he expects violence, even murder. Although he's afraid to leave them alone, he forces himself to go upstairs and finds, to his surprise, that they manage to make up without him!

The more urgent your help seems, the more important it is for you to withhold it for the established time. If a genuine emergency comes up (say, if your pregnant next-door neighbor is alone in the house and starts to go into labor) you can make an exception. But be careful. Real emergencies don't happen often. If you're making a lot of exceptions, you're not giving the exercise a chance.

But what do you tell people who *expect* to borrow your car or who always ask you to do their shopping? As little as possible. You may want to make a simple announcement in advance, or else to say nothing until it comes up.

A friend will be sympathetic if you explain your own need and its urgency. You need a *period of doing no favors*. It's important for you to know that your relationships don't depend on them. And if the person continues calling you selfish and unfair, you'll have to reconsider how sympathetic the person really is.

Above all, don't make the explanations themselves acts of fear. Don't give anyone elaborate reasons for stopping the favors. If you even start *thinking* of elaborate reasons, it's a sign that you're not stopping a minute too soon.

This doesn't mean that you have to tell your friend he's been ruthless and manipulative, unless you're sure you want to. It's usually better to say that you're trying to straighten out your own life, and that part of it's teaching yourself that you don't have to do favors to keep your friends. A well-meaning person should understand.

If a friend is extremely worried about the possibility of an emergency coming up, tell him that you'll help in a critical situation. But don't do this unless you're convinced it's absolutely necessary, and then hold fast. People who specialize in taking favors are experts at inventing emergencies—and have more than their share of real ones besides.

You might find an unpleasant truth or two. Stopping favors can be a frighteningly direct route to discovering problems in a relationship. But the problems are *there*, you're not inventing them, and it's better to know this than go to on deluding yourself by buying someone's friendship.

The exchange of favors should be a secondary aspect of friendship, since it won't mean anything without a genuine alliance. Ideally, a friendship should be capable of surviving without any favors on either side. And even an imperfect friendship—if it *is* a friendship—should easily survive a few "favorless" weeks.

Besides, generosity can be a great pleasure. There are times when we *want* to help others who might otherwise suffer or be less comfortable. People who always do favors out of fear deprive themselves of this pleasure; they only feel pressured, used, insecure. Once you learn when *not* to help people out, you can start getting the most from your own good deeds.

HOW (AND WHY) TO STOP FEELING SORRY FOR YOURSELF 22

Some of us have no idea what's wrong with our lives. Others think they know but don't.

"I had to quit school at seventeen to support my brother," explains Hank. "I never got a chance."

"I had polio as a kid," Elsa is quick to tell you. "I can't walk as well as other people. You can't expect me to get such good jobs."

"You know," confides Joan, "I'm getting old. I can't help it if my life is empty."

Two of the phrases here—"you can't expect me" and "I can't help it if"—are sure-fire signs of self-pity. There are other signs: talking too much about your problems, *thinking* all the time about your problems, campaigning for people's sympathy. "Nobody knows the trouble I've seen" is one of the most common refrains in the world.

In the course of living, everyone runs into real trouble—and some people run into a great deal. We all know people who've been genuine victims of circumstances: they've been ill, lost their loved ones or house or job; they've had physical handicaps or just bad luck. You can't blame them for feeling a little bit sorry for themselves.

Or can you? What is your honest reaction to someone

187

who's always wailing about his circumstances? Chances are, your sympathy gets worn out before long. Eventually, you'd like him to pull himself together—or just to go away.

That's the first problem with self-pity. It's annoying to others. People may be very kind for a while, but sooner or later they're likely to get irritated. Relatives and close friends will probably stick around, but it's easy to see that it's out of a sense of duty. And others may start avoiding the one who's always going on about his hard luck. It's too depressing to talk to him. And there doesn't seem to be a real way to help.

People who get sick and tired of listening to self-pity aren't heartless—they're just responding to a fact of life. And that fact, which is the second big problem with self-pity, is that self-pity is always a dead end. It invites you to stand still and ask "Why me?" instead of figuring out the best place to go from here. It's based on—and keeps reinforcing—the idea that you're helpless. Passive. That everything's been *done* to you, and there's no way you can possibly help yourself. Which is never true and never useful. You *can* help yourself. But only if you stop feeling sorry for yourself first.

To find out just how big a problem this is for you, try the following test. For three weeks, *don't* (1) mention any of your problems to anyone, (2) blame anyone or anything for your situation, or (3) say a word about the way other people have it better than you do. At the same time, *do* take part in and talk about activities that you enjoy.

If you can do these things fairly easily, you shouldn't have much trouble with self-pity. But if you find it hard—or even impossible—to stick it out for three weeks, you're probably going through withdrawal pains. Which is a sign that self-pity is an important part of your life.

How did it get that way? As usual, childhood's a good place for things like this to start. Take Elsa, who came down with polio at age seven. She was very sick and ended up with a permanent, noticeable limp. Everyone—her parents, her teachers, her sisters—felt sorry for her. "What's going to happen," she heard them wonder, "when the poor girl grows up?"

The other kids in school weren't always so sympathetic. She couldn't run or even walk very fast, so they tended to leave her out of their games. Her parents tried to help by giving Elsa expensive toys that the other children would want to play with, and by throwing fabulous parties for her birthday.

Without realizing it, she drew two conclusions from all this: first, that she could always count on love from her family whenever she mentioned her handicap, and second, that people would love her *only* if they felt sorry for her or if she had something they wanted.

Elsa's polio was a trauma—it changed her life. But only because she and her parents *made* it a trauma. Because they believed that a girl couldn't limp and still lead a normal life, they acted in ways that reinforced the belief and eventually made it come true. Before changing—when she was in her thirties—she clung to the premise that helplessness was the only thing she possessed that would serve her.

Self-pity can start with a real misfortune, like Elsa's polio, or it can start with something much more minor. Jody doesn't get straight A's all the time, so she gives up on her plans to be a lawyer. She decides that she'd better just settle for a job as a legal secretary.

Tod isn't good at sports. He feels that everyone must be laughing at him, so he decides to join in the laughter. He becomes the class clown—and every time he laughs at himself he reinforces the idea that he's worthless. That no one could possibly like him unless he put on a good show.

Lance's parents worry and make a fuss over him every time he gets sick, even though he's never had a serious illness. He likes the cookies and sympathy, and he starts exaggerating his symptoms. Eventually, he becomes a hypochondriac and a master at self-pity. He "doesn't feel well enough" to do most things—so he gets most of his satisfaction out of other people's sympathy.

And it's never enough. People are never concerned *enough* about him. No one is impressed *enough* by all he's suffered. Every time he makes a play for sympathy, he reinforces his need for it—and the need becomes impossible to fill. At the same time, he's wasting his life by not striving for anything much *besides* sympathy.

Every one of these people—Elsa, Jody, Tod, Lance—feels that he or she has a tragic flaw, one defect that disqualifies him or her from happiness and success. For Elsa it's the limp; for Jody, stupidity (and she is far from stupid); for Tod, being non-athletic; for Lance, general sickliness. Some of these handicaps are real, some more or less imagined. But it works exactly the same way for both; a handicap is what you make of it. If you have a real liability—if, say, you're blind or have lost a limb or are suffering from a terrible illness—the *chances* of feeling sorry for yourself are increased, because you'll have lots of encouragement from other people. But it's not the only possible response—and it's certainly not the best one.

If you're a self-pitier, figure out what you regard as your handicap. Very likely you know what it is and you talk about it much too often. Stop. See what horrible "truth" about yourself comes to mind in the three weeks when you're not fishing for sympathy. Once you realize what it is you see as your defect, you're in a position to stop letting it run your life.

The way to do this is to act, as much as possible, as if you were not handicapped. Because every time you behave otherwise, every time you act helpless or unworthy, you strengthen your own belief that there is something shamefully wrong with you.

In particular, watch out for—and avoid—the following

six habits. They are especially applicable when you feel that *your* obstacles are insurmountable.

1. **Don't let people attack you or take advantage of you.** Let's say you've lost your job and are spending a lot of time around the house. Don't let your spouse or your parents tell you how inconvenient this is and how lucky you are to have them supporting you.

   "Okay," you might say, "but what if I've gotten sick and *am* a real burden to everyone. Shouldn't I try to to make it up to them?"

   No. These people are supposed to care about you. Ask them not to hold your condition—which is probably temporary and definitely no fault of your own—against you. If they can't agree to this, try to make other living arrangements. But don't start a program of appeasement no matter what; be pleasant and cooperative, but no more. Otherwise, you're telling yourself—more than anyone else can—that what's happened is a disaster that has lowered your worth as a human being. And that message just isn't true.

2. **Don't curtail your aspirations.** Maybe you already have. You decided that since your family was poor or you were deaf in one ear that you couldn't hope to accomplish much. So you never really tried—and hence reinforced the idea that you were incompetent.

   You can start reversing this process. Next time you feel you'd like to do something—whether to learn something or go somewhere or try for a good job—force yourself to try your best. It can be the first step in moving from self-pity to self-respect.

3. **Don't apologize for your handicap.** Bess suffered a broken hip and spent months in bed. The whole time she kept saying she was sorry: to her husband, her children, her visitors. She apologized for the cost of the doctors, the state of the house, and not being able to do the Christmas baking. All of which reinforced her belief that the accident would ruin her whole life. And that she'd somehow done something wrong. Note: I'm not saying never express gratitude. But even then be careful; make it brief. An unending posture of gratitude does its own damage to you and the relationship.

4. **Don't become the household slave:** cooking, sewing, cleaning, babysitting on demand. The premise behind all this is that you're no good and should be grateful for not being kicked out in the street. And the premise gets stronger each time you act on it.

5. **Don't attack yourself for what you see as your defect.** I knew a man who was five foot three and always called himself "Little Charlie." He was skeptical when I first told him that I was sure this habit—and the resultant self-pity—was doing him much more harm than his actual height ever could. But after a few months of making a number of adjustments, in particular, not uttering the words, "Little Charlie," he learned to stop worrying about his height and get on with his life.

6. **Don't pay unnecessary penalties for the handicap.** In the days before contact lenses, many women saw the world as a blur because they refused to wear glasses. Which (a) vastly increased the hardship of their poor eyesight,

and (b) just as important, decreased their sense of self-worth. By reinforcing the myth that if—horrors—they were seen with glasses, no man could possibly love them.

Sit down and take stock of what the handicap will necessarily cost you. Figure out what your limitations are—and aren't. On the one hand, don't keep yourself from pursuing any reasonable goal. But also don't get your heart set on the impossible. If you stutter, don't decide you can be happy only as a radio announcer. The refusal to face a fact of life makes it seem much more horrible than it really is. And makes the one thing you *can't* do much more important than everything you can.

If you try too hard to compensate for a handicap, an interesting thing can happen. Maybe you tell yourself, "If only I didn't have this one flaw, everything would be marvelous." You put all your energy into overcoming that flaw. And what happens? You can actually wipe out a physical handicap—and like yourself less than ever.

It happened to Irving. He was a scrawny teen-ager who was tortured by the way he looked. He decided that weight training was the answer to all his problems and spent hours and hours working out. Eventually, he developed a powerful body. His "handicap" didn't exist anymore, but predictably he became *more* obsessed with looks and physical power. He was terrified of getting old or sick or hurt in any way. So his old fear, his old sense of inadequacy, had more of a grip than ever on him.

Not that you shouldn't strive for improvement. If you can learn to speak without stuttering or learn how to look younger, wonderful. But don't see it as rescuing you from a fate worse than death. And don't expect it to solve all your problems. The antidote is to invest efforts in the pursuit of other goals too. Don't put all of your efforts in one basket.

Get in touch with the feeling that there's nothing wrong with you *now*, as you are at this minute. Suppose you felt that way all the time. How would you act? Act that way. Do nothing to compensate for your flaws—only positive things that can bring you pleasure and strength and achievement. Don't assume there's anything you can't do, unless it's *directly* ruled out by some handicap. And always look for the things that you can do—and do well. Then do them. If you *act* on the idea that you're competent and worthwhile, you'll start to believe in yourself.

ENJOY OLD AGE HOW TO 23

A few words here on the realization that you're getting old.

We're all getting old, of course. A twenty-two-year-old wrote an article recently about the blight of not being a radiant teen-ager any more. And an eighty-two-year-old can genuinely find there are things he can't do as well as he used to.

Rose was seventy-four and demoralized. She felt that she had no future, no real place in anyone's life. That she didn't fit in: on the one hand, she "couldn't stand old people"; on the other, she was sure young people couldn't stand *her*.

We figured out that five basic things were bothering her—and might well bother anyone who feels himself getting old. These were (1) erosion of physical appearance and strength; (2) other people's prejudices against the aged; (3) unwillingness to accept increased dependency on others; (4) the loss of certain friends and loved ones, and (5) the approach of death. All these problems, Rose argued, were impossible to overcome.

But, at my request, we tried to work out a helpful approach anyway. As a start, I suggested that Rose ask herself the following ten questions:

1. In what ways do you discriminate against other old people? For instance, do you condemn your husband as a "poor old man" or talk differently to older people from the way you do to younger ones? Do you say that other people your age who try to have a good time are making fools of themselves?

2. Do you have ways of buying friendship from younger people? Volunteering gifts and services you'd never expect them to offer you?

3. What dispensations do you grant the young —and not yourself? Do you, for example, always show up on time, but "understand that the young people have better things to do"?

4. Do you believe you're too old to understand certain things (politics, perhaps, or unisex clothes or the new movies)? And do you use this as an excuse not to pay attention to what's going on around you?

5. Do you conceal your personal problems because you feel you have no right to bother young people?

6. Do you try to establish yourself as an expert on life and give constant advice to young people?

7. Do you dwell on the past and ask sympathy because your life is over?

8. Do you criticize the modern world, calling it immoral or decaying? Do you maintain that you have no place in it?

9. Do you invade the privacy of the young, trying to live their lives instead of talking and thinking about your own?

10. Do you demand that young people listen to long speeches that you make—and get upset

if they interrupt? Are you really listening to what they say?

These are all ways in which an older person might discriminate against older people (and thus poison his mind about himself) or ask indulgence because he's too old to be held responsible. *And they're all ways an older person might keep reinforcing the idea that old people— starting with him—are no good.*

Rose realized, among other things, that she was ashamed of her husband, who used a walker to get about. She tended to pick on him, particularly if there were younger people around. "Can't you hurry *up*? We're keeping the kids waiting."

She also recognized all the favors she did for her children—and the way she wouldn't accept any favors or even appreciation from them in return. "Don't thank me," she always said. "I'm your mother."

Finally, she saw that she belittled herself as much as her husband. "You'll have to excuse me. I'm just an old woman." Simultaneously, she usually managed to ask for sympathy: "A lot of my friends are gone. I don't have much more time."

Once she recognized some of these patterns in her life, Rose could hardly wait to change them. She loved her husband and didn't really want to embarrass him; she had just gotten in the habit of being so ashamed of old age that she felt embarrassed *for* him. Once she stopped putting him down, it was easier to stop putting herself down—and also easier to believe that their age was no disgrace.

I suggested she cut down on favors—and start making plans of her own. She hadn't gone out on weekends for years; she wanted to be available "in case the children need me." One of her hardest decisions was the resolution to book herself solid on weekends for a whole month—and stick to her appointments. After so many years of refusing to do things for herself, it was time she started.

One of the things Rose started was a class in gardening, which was an old hobby. This helped turn her thinking around, from the belief that "it's all downhill from now on" to the idea that she could still do new things, make new progress.

At this point we looked back at the five impossible problems of old age. They were still real difficulties, but Rose had certain ideas for coping with them successfully. For example, we talked about the problem of losing good looks and perfect health. For Rose, this was worse than it had to be. She'd stopped taking care of herself shortly after she turned forty. "What's the point?" she figured.

Now, at seventy-four, Rose decided there *was* some point. Not in trying to look forty again—that would backfire and make her more ashamed of getting older. Just as buying a toupee is probably the worst way for a man to adjust to baldness. But Rose made up her mind to buy some new clothes, get her hair done, go for a long walk now and then for exercise. And she started looking for ways not to let other physical limitations stop her—for instance, buying a magnifying glass to help her read recipes instead of just giving up on cooking.

As for prejudice against old people, the decision she'd already made—not to participate in it herself—gave her a sense of perspective. While she recognized that there would always be some people who were prejudiced against the aged (frequently because *they* dreaded growing old), she stopped assuming that everyone hated old people and—more important—that such hatred was justified.

And she decided that being a little dependent on her friends and children wasn't all that terrible after all. She'd done a lot for them in the past forty-five years, and they honestly wanted to act generously in return. But she was making it as hard as possible, sometimes acting as if an offer to drive her somewhere or run an errand were an insult instead of a favor. And always bringing out the self-pity: "I'm so old; I'm such a bother."

It wasn't easy for her, but Rose managed to force herself to start accepting favors—and accepting graciously. Once she did it, her horror about the idea went away, and she actually found it was pleasant to know that some people cared enough to go out of their way for her.

Rose's parents were dead; so were her brothers, some cousins, and friends. One of her sisters was dying. She associated these people with youth and with good times; there was reason to mourn their passing.

But not reason to turn it into a trauma, to refuse to enjoy life from that day on. After her favorite brother died, Rose had gone into permanent, if low-key, mourning. Around this time she stopped going out and making plans for the future. She eventually came to see that this was not an inevitable, proper, concerned response—but a choice, and an overreaction. At first, when she started to rejoin the world, she felt a vague sense that she was betraying her brother. But she also realized that he wouldn't have approved of the kind of person she'd turned herself into. He had been in his seventies when he died—and much younger somehow than she was now. Perhaps it made sense to become more like him, instead of acting only half alive.

As she faced up to her brother's death, Rose started thinking and talking openly for the first time about the idea of her own death. Which didn't magically remove all fear and sorrow, but *did* reduce the terror of the very thought. This is probably the most important lesson that self creation can teach us: *Refusing to face something— anything—always makes it much, much worse.* Admitting that you will die—not refusing to think about it or pretending that your children give you immortality—can give you a sense of your own courage, and an impulse to make the most of your life right now.

It took some time for Rose to work all this out, but

she did it. Even though she started at age seventy-four—and she believed at first that she was too old to do *anything* new—she managed to change her whole life. It is easier if you start young. But it's never too late to give life new promise.

WHAT TO DO ABOUT SHYNESS 24

Imagine yourself at a cocktail party where you know only a few people. You've talked to those people, who've then moved off to get fresh drinks or talk to other friends. You see a group that you think you might like to join. What do you do now? Walk up, smile, and introduce yourself? Stand on the edge of the group and hope to be noticed? Go off in search of the people you already know? Or try to think of an urgent reason why you should leave the party?

If it sounds hard to introduce yourself to new people —even at a party, where you're *supposed* to be meeting new people—you're probably shy. Like millions of people, you're a little afraid of strangers—maybe even of people you know. Perhaps parties are the worst for you. Or a situation where you have something big at stake: a job interview or a meeting with potential in-laws. Or perhaps shyness holds you back almost all the time. You've worked somewhere for a few months, and you'd like to start seeing some of the people outside the office, but you're too shy to suggest it. Or you don't know how to approach a man or woman you find attractive. Or you dread seeing your doctor or having your hair cut because you're not sure what to say to people.

Shyness can take an extreme form. Outside London, a woman named Alice Neville heads a group called The Open Door. This group rarely meets, although many members live near one another. The members stay home and read the newsletter. If they're lucky, they're able to talk to each other on the phone. If they're very lucky, they can pay a visit to Mrs. Neville. Lucky? Yes, because all of these people are afraid of joining the outside world.

Some years ago, Mrs. Neville wrote a magazine article describing her own struggle with what she called agoraphobia—a fear of open spaces. Her symptoms? She dreaded going outside, talking to strangers, even meeting the necessary people to take care of routine chores and business. More and more she found herself withdrawing—staying home, not going out, not meeting people. Until she recognized what was going on—and decided to fight it. After a desperate effort, she managed to conquer the fear.

Mrs. Neville had written articles before, and she was used to a few readers writing in. This time thousands wrote, saying "I have the same problem." Some suffered mildly, avoiding social events and finding it hard to talk to anyone who wasn't an old and trusted friend. Others stayed home almost all the time. They had mates or children do the shopping. They would only go out after dark or in a car with the windows rolled up. Some were afraid to answer the door or even to pick up the phone when it rang.

Most of these people, Mrs. Neville realized, also suffered from another fear—the fear of having to be in *any* particular place for any reason. They wanted to be able to leave company at any moment, but they were almost equally afraid of having to stay alone.

What helps? Mrs. Neville has found that psychoanalysis seldom does. Looking for roots isn't the answer. Many patients use their analysis as an excuse not to face the world: "I can't go out and meet people until I've worked through these problems." And they actually end up more frightened and dependent.

What helps is to stop reinforcing the fear by ceasing to act on it. Go to a party or ask the landlord to get the place painted or start lining up interviews for a better job —anything that you've been avoiding out of fear. Mrs. Neville did it, even when her fear was so strong that it seemed impossible. And now she advises others, "You must try to increase the radius of your activities by forcing yourself."

The Principle shows us where shyness comes from— and why forcing yourself is the only way to beat it. *Shyness is a habit that starts in various ways but always gets reinforced in the same way: by acting on it.*

Sometimes it starts with a physical illness. Amanda had recently moved to a new city when she came down with pneumonia and complications. By the time she felt completely well, she had started to think, "Well, I've been here six months, and I haven't made any real friends, so I guess that I'm not going to." And then she made it come true. She felt fine now, but she'd gotten used to quiet evenings at home. It would be a bit of a jolt to go out, stay out late, take a chance with new people. Why take that chance? So she turned down most invitations to go anywhere. It would be too hot, too cold, too tiring, she told herself. And every time she did this, she was also telling herself that it was an ordeal to make friends. It was hopeless. She wouldn't know how to act. Everyone would think she was boring. Or clumsy. Or stupid. They wouldn't like her.

Amanda turned her illness into a trauma that made her shy. Other people get goaded into shyness by their parents. Morris, for instance, had very shy parents who loved him fiercely and taught him the difference between family, whom you could trust, and everyone else, whom you couldn't. He imitated his parents' shyness when he was young and kept on acting the same way as he got older. And he kept on *feeling* the same way as a result.

Nina's parents weren't shy at all, but they encouraged her to be. She was the only girl in a large family; girls, she was constantly told, should be quiet, polite, and tidy. They shouldn't put themselves forward. The more Nina practiced what her parents preached—the more she acted shy—the more she taught herself to *be* shy and unassertive.

Becky's parents prompted her to be shy in still a different way. They were loud, aggressive, pushy. One time they pushed past guards and thrust Becky in front of Rita Hayworth to get an autograph. Becky, who admired the film star, was mortified. Telling herself, "I don't want to make a fool of myself the way they do," she set out to act as *differently* from her parents as she could.

Amanda, Morris, Nina, and Becky all created their shyness—and kept re-creating it because they kept acting on it. Like all habits, it felt natural and inevitable to them. But they had to ignore that feeling and break the habit—by making themselves do the things they were afraid to do.

This is the only way anyone can break out of shyness. You have to seek out human contacts and force yourself to make the most of them. You can't make excuses to leave, or sit there quietly and watch the clock, or try to get someone else to come along for moral support. You simply have to go through with it: meeting people.

And it isn't so bad. You've been missing a lot through shyness. And you've been reinforcing the idea that people are frightening, that you live in a frightening world. Think about this. What is so terrifying? Only action will drive the fear away, but it may help you to make a start if you do some thinking along these lines:

1. Think first about what you have in common with all people. Human frailty, susceptibility

to disease, the desire for friendship and respect, even the fear of death. Everyone has these. No matter how high and mighty someone seems, he is vulnerable like you. Truly accomplished people, those with the courage to look into themselves, recognize this. They know that they're made from the same stuff as you are. And you should know this too.

2. Take stock of your strengths and interests. Try to meet people—at least some of the time —in the context of things you do well and enjoy doing. Note how you act in this context. It may be that the only place you're comfortable with others is in your own kitchen. Or you're a Ping-Pong champ who's shy any place but the Ping-Pong parlor. In either case, watch how you behave there. What's different? Do you like yourself better? Maybe you can copy your own style when you approach people in other situations.

3. Guard against elitism in any form. If you think some people are beneath you—someone at work, your brother-in-law, a bad Ping-Pong player—you are setting yourself up to be afraid to approach others. After all, they might look down on you in the same way. By snobbery you reinforce the belief that only successful people have a right to personal confidence. Instead you need to create the premise that everyone—including you—has a right to be treated with respect.

The opposite of elitism is the belief that you are a citizen of the world, and so is everyone else. There is no such thing as a "right family" or a wrong one. Money, neighborhood, profession, power—none of these gives you the right to look down on others. *Or gives it to anyone else.* No one is entitled to laugh at you or act as if you're not good enough for him.

4. Avoid rationalizations that say the time and place are wrong for you to put yourself forward. When you're shy, you always feel like an intruder; it always seems that the time isn't right. At a social gathering, it may help to imagine you'll be there forever. Pretend you'll *never* meet anyone else; this group is your universe. You need a friend in it. And other people do too.

5. Think about the people who frighten you most. What are they like? Do they fit into a special class—young or attractive or rich or successful in some special way? What makes you single them out?

You may find that you're not really interested in these people; you just admire their youth or looks or glamorous lives. You'd like to be able to say that you talked to someone famous. In such cases you may be shy because you sense the fraud underlying your interest. If the other person knew the truth, he or she would avoid you and would be right to do so.

The kind of shyness we want to beat is the kind that is holding you back from the people who do interest you. And you know how to beat it. Stop running away— go where you will meet people, then stay and talk to them. Seek out groups as often as possible, and follow these suggestions:

1. **Try to sit in the center of the room.** Shy people often put themselves in a corner so that they'll be overlooked. It works; no one

notices them. Which "proves" that no one really cares, and so on—in a vicious cycle. Break it. Give other people a chance to notice and care about you.

2. **Speak up.** People who secretly want to disappear and not take part in a group tend to speak in muffled tones. Raise your voice, and you'll reinforce the idea that you have the right to speak.

3. **Look at people when they talk to you.** People who are shy often forget that they owe other people this much acknowledgment. It isn't necessary to stare at people. But it's important for them to know that you're listening. And looking at them will help you to believe your response will be taken seriously.

4. **Repeat yourself if you aren't answered.** Don't create the excuse for yourself that people aren't interested in what you say.

5. **Finish what you say even if you are interrupted.** We all get interrupted, and shy people sometimes invite interruptions by acting as if they expect to be cut off. But interruptions can also mean that people are getting excited about the things you're saying. Don't use an interruption as an excuse to withdraw from the group.

Is it this simple—look at people, speak up? Yes. Without realizing it, shy people almost never do look at people or speak loud enough, and acts like these are what keep them shy.

You'll feel anxious at first, as you always do when you change a pattern. You still see yourself in the old way—it seems preposterous to raise your voice or return to a topic you initiated. You may feel as if you suddenly resemble a parent whose pushiness embarrassed you. With the method of magnification, you can take a good look at your fears. But the most important thing is to keep going despite those fears. Act differently and you will see yourself differently.

You can work up to some of this gradually if you like. Sure, it would do wonders for your shyness to make a speech. But right now, you find it almost impossible to go into the street without a close friend at your side. Then start by speaking louder and looking directly at that one friend. Create habits with a few people that you can carry over to others later. Strengthen yourself little by little. Even in a room with one other person, you can increase your sense of freedom and confidence. Go to a party when you can, and start by concentrating on people who seem receptive. Approach them first, and gradually try to work around to some people you don't know at all.

If you know for sure some comment you will want to make *and will have a chance* to make, rehearse it to yourself prior to the gathering. But don't memorize random remarks on subjects you cannot be sure will arise to be dropped into a forthcoming discussion: You'll spend all your time anxiously looking for the apt moment to play your three trumps. If the apt moment doesn't come, you'll either (a) force the remarks inappropriately, or (b) end up saying nothing because your recorded-message posture has made it impossible for you to respond spontaneously. Remarks are made to which you in fact have a pertinent ad-lib, but your ad-lib speaker has been disconnected.

Remember: It's not a question of finding the courage to speak, but of speaking to find the courage. You don't need specific courage to take the first step. You only need the meta-courage that comes from belief in the self creation principle. Many a person in training has said to his coach, "I can't do that!" and the coach has responded, "You can. Trust me. Try." And they try. And they do it. Not wholly out of trust in themselves, but trust in their coach. But thereafter they do trust themselves.

In our case the coach is the self creation principle. It says, "You can do it. Try." If you trust the Principle, you'll soon trust yourself.

CREATIVITY: ITS CARE AND NURTURE **25**

This chapter is addressed to those people who are creative—but have trouble *creating*. If you have a talent and an urge to pursue it, the Principle will help ensure that your talent is given its best chance. It tells you the sorts of acts to avoid and the ones to pursue if you want to maintain the openness, sensitivity, courage, and application that comprise the optimal soil for creative work. The Principle can help you to stay on course in your work. Here are some guidelines:

1. **At least some of the time, do work that's for your eyes only.** Once you realize that no one —ever—will be judging the work, you'll feel freer to take chances, to be original. There are people who find it difficult even to write frankly in a private journal, because they think, "What if someone peeked at it?" or "What if I get to be famous someday and it's published?" Don't let this happen to you: Promise yourself that certain works will be private, and ask your family and friends to respect this.

2. **Guard against other acts that can make rep-**

utation or success too important to you. I know a professional writer who gets good advances for his books, but he spends the money fast and then feels he "owes" the manuscript. It isn't his anymore.

You don't need to be a professional to create the same kind of pressure. Maybe you tell everyone about this fantastic project you're working on—it'll be the best thing they've ever seen. So your friends start asking how it's coming along and when they'll be able to see it and—eventually—why it's taking so long. You start to feel, like the writer I mentioned, that you have this debt to your public.

Convince yourself that your work is for *you* by not trying to do a hard-sell to others. Remember the Principle: The more you concern yourself with other people's opinions, the more important those opinions will become to you. If you carry this to extremes—say, by trying to use a splashy success as an artist to make up for a lifetime of other failures—you can make yourself feel so much pressure that you can't work at all. But the less you look to others for applause, the more freedom and confidence you'll start to feel.

3. **Set up a *realistic* schedule and stick to it.** If you schedule six days a week for your project, and you haven't been working two, you aren't likely to hold to it. Which is dangerous: Every time you fail to live up to your schedule, you make yourself feel less up to the work. This is especially true if the work isn't going too well—which is when you're most likely to abandon a difficult schedule.

Impose a reasonable discipline on yourself, a work schedule that you can live with. Perhaps you dislike the idea of tying yourself down to specific times; you'd rather work when you feel inspired. But then what happens when you hit a dry spell—and a week passes with no inspiration? You can make yourself lose faith in your capacity to work.

At least at the start, you can help yourself by programming a few hours to be alone to try your specialty. Sticking to a schedule will help you to do more work—if you want to be working in the first place.

If the schedule you've set for yourself isn't too harsh, but you find yourself fighting it—making excuses to break it—you can learn something about your motives. Schedules force you to ask the hard question: *Do I really want to do this—to stick to it even when it's not going too well?* If the answer is No, fine. Why feel like a delinquent because you're not an artist if you don't really want to be one? But if the answer is Yes, if you really do want to do this, you'll find that the schedule will help you get past any creative lulls.

4. **Sacrifice for your work.** Once you've scheduled time for your project, don't use that time to talk on the phone or cook an elaborate dinner or take in a movie on television.

A would-be composer found that she constantly took away from her time to write by scheduling lunches with friends. While she wouldn't think of canceling an appointment with one friend to see another, it never occurred to her to honor an appointment with herself in the same way. As the Principle advises, make your work important by investing in the basic arrangements to do it.

5. **Keep trying, especially after criticism that hurts.** Don't turn failures of any kind into traumas. If you keep at your work, you renew your belief in yourself and in the importance of creativity in your life. Even working badly is almost always better than not working.

"One must fire on the target," said the writer Stendhal. If you don't—and if you don't *keep* firing on that target—you'll not only lose confidence but may also start to forget that there *is* a target. You quit trying to write—and find yourself wondering why you wanted to be a poet in the first place and how you got the idea that you had a chance.

There's another kind of quitting to watch out for. Every time you have trouble with a poem, you rush to do some other creative work—photography, perhaps, or model-making. (After all, you think, it's constructive. . . .) It's fine to have two projects, but never use difficulty with one as an excuse to turn to the other. If you do, you'll make yourself lose confidence—and competence—in both.

6. **Finish projects if you possibly can, even if you don't like the way they're turning out.** When you finish something, you reinforce the idea that you're serious about your work, that you're someone who sees things through. Not finishing can make you see yourself as a quitter. And it gets harder to start things when you're not sure that you'll ever finish them.

This is important. A creative effort can take a few hours—or it can take years. Either way, you'll come to a point where you have to choose: Will you finish the work or abandon it? It helps to know from the start that you're likely to choose to finish—otherwise, what are you working toward?

If you're a professional, or want to be, you have to go beyond finishing the project itself: You have to make sure that it gets seen and criticized. Don't just send your novel to one publisher and give up if it gets rejected. Send it to many, to ensure that it has its chance. You worked hard on it, sacrificed for it. If you abandon it now, you'll be undermining your commitment to your work.

7. **When you criticize your own work, remember that your moods change.** And your moods are influenced by the criticism you've already done. If you've been correcting a work of art savagely for days and days, you may start to convince yourself that it's no damn good. The more you patch up its defects, the more disqualifying those defects may look to you.

Try this quick test of your mood. If everything you've done in the last month looks just awful to you, it may be that you've turned disparagement into a habit. Stop. Examine the work of some other artists. Often, when you've gotten into the habit of running down your own work, you'll find that you even dislike the work of your favorites. And that's a sign that your judgment is getting distorted.

There's always a danger in criticizing; it's likely to put you in a critical frame of mind. It can teach you to think small, inhibit your creative flow. Try not to stop and revise in the middle of creative work; hold off till the end, or at least till a large segment is done, and then treat criticizing it as a separate project. Each activity—creating, revising —requires its own outlook. And each activity creates its own outlook; as you create, you grow more creative; as you criticize, you get more critical. If you keep them separate, you can keep from reinforcing a fiercely critical attitude when your real project is creating. When you do revise your work, try to think of it as an act of love toward the work. You're improving it, polishing it, reinforcing its virtues. Remove its faults gently. It's because it's worthwhile—not because it's no good— that you are taking the trouble.

Even if you don't like the work, don't turn away from it too quickly to learn from it. If it disgusts you, think about why. How does it fall short of your expectations? If you just try to forget about it—to annihilate the past—you will make yourself feel incompetent. Besides, what you *did* is not the ultimate measure of what you can do.

8. **When you finish something you like, don't brag about it.** You'll probably want to show it to people, especially if you think it's beautiful. Fine—show it by all means. But simply present it. Trying to enhance it by talking it up is an act of fear, which can only make you more afraid. And it doesn't make sense: Your work of art is not a logical argument that needs you to defend it. Allow it to stand alone; it'll help you to stand alone too.

9. **Cultivate the qualities that you will need in your work.** A creative outlook goes beyond

painting or writing or building—it's an attitude toward all of life. To start cultivating this attitude—

- Let yourself be surprised by the different ways that you feel and act. Try not to judge your feelings.
- Cultivate a taste for the absurd in the world around you. Try to appreciate the unusual, instead of criticizing people and ideas as strange.
- Learn to play; do things for no ulterior purpose. You need that capacity in creative work, and you're not likely to have it there if you don't cultivate it anywhere else.
- Again, work against depending on other people's judgments. Don't ask for others' opinions of what you're doing. Don't investigate how well people your age have done in your kind of work. Don't study the market in your field. Forget comparisons—define a successful life as doing the best you possibly can.

Even with these guidelines, creative work has rough moments. Time and again you're going to face anxiety: Am I making progress, is this going to work, where on earth can I go from here? If you *didn't* feel this anxiety, it would probably mean that your work was too safe—that it wasn't really creative.

Every artist on earth goes through this anxiety, yet it usually comes as a shock. Why? Because we don't expect it, and it feels like a sign of trouble. Just as the project seems to be going well, we get a glimpse of all the work, all the pitfalls ahead. It's like looking down from the edge of a cliff; you can fall a long way if you aren't careful. . . .

So it is tempting to be careful. To think, maybe I shouldn't try that new technique after all, but go back to the old one that always worked.

What happens if you give in? First of all, your work suffers; you can't break new ground if you keep retreating to familiar territory. But more important, you reinforce a fear of taking risks—a fear that can wipe out your creativity.

Learn to expect the anxiety; it's a good sign, a sign of creative energy. And expect the temptations that go with it: the impulses to quit, to retrench, to do something safe instead of new. *Then don't give in*; don't act on those temptations. If you resist them, they'll go away, the anxiety will subside, and your work and your confidence will be much stronger.

Creative work can be lonely as well as anxious. If you turn too much to your friends for support and encouragement, you can reinforce too much concern with their reactions. But if you don't, you may feel that you're all alone. . . .

Try to think of a perfect audience—an imaginary community—for your work. Suppose you're making a tapestry that you'd like a friend in another city to see. And a teacher you had a long time ago, and some friends who in fact will see it. Perhaps you like to think that your favorite composer would also walk by and admire it. Imagine this ideal, sympathetic audience—and do the work for them. You owe this community a good, honest effort —your best—and that's all it'll ask of you.

Finally, use your successes wisely. When you've had a good day, try to pinpoint all the ways you felt and acted differently from usual. Maybe you tackled something difficult right at the start instead of trying to work up to it. Or maybe you decided not to take the shortcut you were considering, or not to go to the beach that weekend instead of working. Look for actions that you can repeat the next time to reinforce a positive attitude.

At the same time, be careful not to make so much of a success that you create the fear that you'll never live up to it. Maybe you've been painting for months and rejecting the pictures every time, painting over them. But suddenly, here's the painting you wanted to do; it's wonderful. You put it up in the living room, take snapshots of it, carry the pictures with you everywhere. Sometimes you even tell people it's the only picture you've ever done.

Of course you should enjoy your achievement. But be careful not to overstress it, or hide your failures. If you treat any single accomplishment as a miracle, you can convince yourself that it *was* a miracle—and miracles don't happen too often. Instead, look again at all the actions that helped you work well, and try to keep acting in the same way. Don't let a success undermine the real secret of that success—the work habits that you've developed.

THE STAMP
OF NATURE **26**

What should psychology do? It should enable people to understand and to help themselves. Modern psychology is now a century old, and it hasn't done this. Few if any truths have emerged from it, and no effective system of therapy. The insights of classical analysis were not only false but many were downright harmful: You are in thrall to your past, your psyche is frozen, current action is irrelevant.

But as Fritz Perls wrote, "Therapy oriented to the past is invalid because the *whys* of the patient's neurosis really explain very little. Why does a situation produce neurosis in Mr. A while the same situation leaves Mr. B untouched?"

The self creation principle gives the answer.

Perls also wrote about a troubled man raised by a stern maiden aunt. To say that the aunt sabotaged him, Perls notes, "only gives the patient license to project all difficulties on to his aunt. It gives him a scapegoat, not an answer." In other words, it doesn't tell him how to proceed. It gives him no plan. The mere insight into the childhood relationship does nothing to alter the person. Only a change in action patterns can do that.

What we are responsive to is not relationships in the

past, but actions in the present. All personal feelings and beliefs can be traced to current actions that sustain them.

You can have all the insight in the world about a muscle: its structure, phylogeny, chemistry. But what builds it up, what it is responsive to, is *action*.

It does not belittle the human psyche to explain so much of it with a single principle, any more than Newton's simple formula, displacing a bewildering (and false) complexity of astronomic mystique, belittled the solar system. If that's the way it works, that's the way it works.

And consider the advantages of it. We said that psychology's task should be to give us understanding and control over our lives. Its "truths" should take two forms: (1) general, that is, a principle or principles that account generically for what is going on, and (2) specific, being a catalog of particular do's and don'ts.

The self creation principle does this. The Principle gives the general law explaining how you come by your personal feelings and beliefs. And it directly implies—and this book has tried to state some of them—lists of harmful decisions commonly made by people with a particular problem. And it also predicates the *helpful* decisions in life.

Because it says any decision will strengthen the motivation behind it, it teaches us that the secret to controlling our own lives lies in precisely this: acting on only those ideas and feelings that we want to live with. Those who want to live with fear, tension, greed, or even total vacuity of appetite, have the formula they need. And so do those who choose love, trust, confidence, and zest.

This provision of a principle as well as specifics is what makes self creation uniquely valuable. Several recent popular psychology books have supplied some excellent specific items of advice. But because they lack the explanatory principle, three or four disadvantages ensue.

First, they occasionally offer advice that cannot be effected because it isn't couched in action terms. It's fruitless to urge people to adopt directly moods or convictions: "Relax; tell yourself you've got a right to . . . ; don't be afraid . . . ; tell yourself that you're as good as . . . ." You can tell yourself sweet nothings forever, but if you're engaging in a cluster of activities ultimately based on self-doubt, in the end it will be the self-doubt that prevails, and you'll say, "Why should I listen to me? No one else does."

Second, not infrequently, the advice is categorically wrong. Earlier I cited the faulty tip that, if you want to seem attractive, you should "line the walls with books." It's faulty because the premise behind it is that the true you is not good enough; you must construct a selling package for yourself—but what gets bought is the package, not the contents. Another book advocates as a method of building your trust in someone that you fabricate a false Achilles' tendon to see if the other person attacks it. Since the premise is doubt about the other person, the doubt is intensified regardless of his response. Doubt about people in general is intensified. A sense of savagery in the world is heightened. Suspicion and the need to screen, to test, to keep people at a safe distance—all these are made louder in your head, which was exactly the opposite of what was intended.

One of the major values of the self creation principle is its usefulness in cutting through complicated masquerades to what is the true belief-act-belief chain. A traditional analyst once mentioned a patient who was wracked with a premonition of sexual indiscretion—that she would drive to town and immediately try to seduce the gas station attendant, the grocery store clerk, the corner traffic cop. The analyst was startled when I said, "So she seldom goes to town, and when she does it's in a drab neck-to-ankle dress, she wears no make-up, she drives with the windows up, she adheres to a rigid agenda of minimal stops and purchases, and hurries back home." The description, which the analyst said was accurate, followed directly from the self creation question: Given the fear, what sort of *protection* was being pursued?

The self creation principle is rich with seeming paradoxes like this: Self-protection does not alleviate fear, it *increases* it. But it's exactly when the Principle unmasks "common sense" as common error that it's likely to do the most widespread good.

A third shortcoming in books of often good advice that have no explanatory principle is that if they do not exactly address the specific problem you have, it's guesswork as to what you should do. When the self creation principle is thoroughly understood, it reveals the specific way to proceed in *any* given situation.

Ultimately, self creation is the study of how actions affect you, and thus how to determine which choices to make. The truths of self creation are perhaps what psychology was originally designed to find, and I think all psychology of the future should begin with the Principle.

And not just psychology. Another advantage of the Principle is that it is applicable beyond its field of origin. The superb anthropologist Ruth Benedict said: "Society is personality writ large." A society, a tribe, a nation inculcates its own beliefs by what it does. The self creation principle is totally *culture free*. It applies no matter how far a person or a society is from Vienna. The concept of trauma applies to societies as well as single persons, and it applies uniformly throughout the world: Depression, famine, war—and new riches (from, say, oil), exposure to new cultures, domination by a new leader—all these events are traumas if they lead to an interruption in the nation's previous life-style. But if the new leader, however magnetic, does not foster a new style of action, he will not affect the personality of the state. With the Principle at hand, we can discern precisely why a given society is or was closed, suspicious, stingy, open, liberal, creative, warlike.

History is the study of the self creation of peoples of

the past. The Principle is a new lens through which to view history, and biography too. We can ask such questions as: What did da Vinci *do* that continually destroyed his interest in finishing one masterpiece after another? Suppose like Michelangelo he had fought to keep others from seeing a work before it was finished? This exercise, of looking to a person's or society's actions to understand what and why they believe, is salubrious. It trains one's focus to be where it belongs, because it is always the *actions* that are creating the beliefs. A given tribe is notable for its stinginess, though it lives amidst plenty. Peer into its history and we discover a time of famine and want—but that was long ago. The trouble is that at that time the tribe adopted certain rituals and customary behavior toward goods that survive to this day. They still are in the grip and mood of that time past, not because of some abstract tribal memory or philosophy, but because of current actions. To say they are stingy because they think stingy is to hold the less useful end of the stick. They directly control their own actions, and I maintain that if they change their actions by refraining from acting on stingy motives, the stingy thinking will wither. Don't say they can't change their actions until they change their motives, that is, their thinking, because the fact of the matter is that nobody—no person, no tribe, no nation—has constantly uniform motivating impulses: The stingiest of men will experience a fleeting kind thought. The basic strategy of self creation is to sort through the continuous heterogeneous stream of thoughts, feelings, impulses, inclinations, and *fish from that stream only those you want strengthened—and act on them.*

Each time you act on a fish from that stream, you add a fraction to its size. And though at the outset the species you're angling for—say, confidence—is minnow-like, if you keep acting on it, and passing by the guppies of self-doubt, you'll eventually have the stream stocked the way you want it.

The key to the usefulness of self creation as a therapy lies in exactly this: You can command your actions; you cannot command your emotions.

The implications of the self creation principle are endless. Let's review a few of the insights it yields, some of which we've already mentioned:

- An "insight" is a perception of the impact on yourself of an act through perceiving the true motive for the act and realizing you are intensifying that motive.

- You are never *taught* an attitude, by parents or anyone else. You are *exposed* to it, but only your own actions bring it inside you, make you feel it. No matter what people drum into you, you only believe it if you act on it.

- It's important to diversify your personal investments. If a single object, task, or person occupies you totally, to the exclusion of everything else, you are in peril. A new lover or spouse should not lead you to forsake all other friends or interests. Nor should a new job or hobby do this. If you're on a long, important project, it's helpful to have an idea what you'd like your *next* project to be—not to distract you from this one, but to ensure that you keep going in life. You can take a well-needed rest, but if you don't get moving again, the finish of the first project can be a trauma: an interruption, or even termination, of a life-style. This is particularly so if the big project is not a success. Anthony Trollope used to put a newly completed novel in a drawer for six months before delivering the manuscript because he wanted to be well into his next work when the first was published. That way the impact of an unfavorable reception was lessened a great deal. I don't recommend fearfully hiding the fruits of your labor, but you should see to it that you don't feel your life stands or falls upon the success of a single effort. This isn't to say don't make *big* investments; the key is, don't make *just one* investment.

- Parents will love their children to the extent that they do for them. But it also follows that children will love their parents to that extent *they* do for *them,* so do not excuse your children from all service and courtesy.

- But motivating children by punishment will only increase their fear and desire to avoid pain. Always try to see that children—or anyone—are enticed to action by a beneficial motive. If the aim is to get them to take dance lessons, first expose them to delightful ballet performances so that their motivation is *to be able to do that,* and not simply to avoid chastisement if they don't practice.

- It follows too that the use of ulterior rewards is dangerous. "I'll give you a dollar if you do your piano exercises," or ". . . if you drive me to the station." What gets reinforced here is the desire for the reward, not affection for the piano or for you.

- All of this means that *behaviorism,* the psychology popularized by B. F. Skinner, is a disaster. As the philosopher John Searle has phrased it, "Behaviorism is incompetent to deal with, analyze, explain human behavior because it does not recognize *intention,* which is essential [to human acts]." Self creation says that it's *not in the reward or punishment but in the striving* that you re-create yourself. It's the *choosing,* the pursuit of motive, that makes for change or reinforcement. What does an act reinforce? A feeling, a conviction. But the behaviorist will not deal with such things, because he cannot observe your feelings, only your behavior. But you *are* interested in your feelings. Behaviorism is wrong in believing the critical moment *follows* the act. It is blind to motive. It cannot cope at all with the "functional autonomy" of habits, and in some sense *habits* are what self creation is all about.

- Self creation gives us an entirely new insight into and appreciation of our actions in general. This is obviously useful, but is also fascinating. Acts of self-protection, pretense, giving, competition—whatever—can now be understood and evaluated in terms of the motive behind them. For our purposes, no act is intrinsically good or bad, harmful or beneficial, only motives are. (This is not to say your acts can't be harmful to *others*. You must not be indifferent to such harm. I'm not of the school that thinks the only measure of an act is the pleasure it gives the actor. And yet I do believe that a persuasive argument against callousness toward others can be made in terms of its ultimate harmful effect on you.) Take the four acts above. One can imagine instances of *self-protection* that are good, not just because they save your life but because they build your self-esteem; or *pretense* that is good because the entire motivation is to comfort another and not to win approval for yourself; or *giving* that is bad because it's motivated by fear; or *competition* that is good because it has a premise of confidence, of belief that you are not an invalid. An awareness of the self creation principle allows us to see the price we're paying for each purchase we make. If we do *this* in order to acquire or achieve *that*, the price will be an increase in this motivating feeling or belief. In our psyches, we are all independent grown-ups; no one else can pay our bills.

That brings us back to the basic message of this book. You are responsible for your own life.

Every personal feeling or belief, every attitude toward yourself, toward others, toward the threats and promises of the world, is put there by you.

I don't mean there are no unfair legacies at birth—poverty, infirmity, prejudice against you—but I do mean that your attitude toward these conditions is created entirely by you.

Nor do I mean that outrage is never appropriate, fear never justified, dismay never rational. What this book is intended to do is to help you to dispel the unwarranted and unnecessary miseries of life, and to generate the joys, love and satisfactions that are available to us. They are available, but not guaranteed. Only you can make them happen.

You are responsible for your own life. Right now you are making it what it is. I see this not as a message of indictment, but of hope. Nothing is frozen in your personality—no form of shame or guilt or anxiety, no form of confidence. It's all subject to change, no matter what your age, no matter what your predicament. Like every other human being, you have power over your opinion of yourself, over your values, and over your view of life. Little by little you can alter any atittude you hold, if you know which choices to make.

Admittedly this means the criminal is responsible for his criminality, the desperate for their desperation, the mean, the vicious, and the selfish for their ugliness. I believe this. Being an analyst does not mean that one thinks nothing in mankind is contemptible. But it does mean—if one is a self creation analyst—that one believes in mutability, remedy, hope.

There is always some place to start. *Always*. In the myriad rivers of emotion, idea, and impulse that comprise your consciousness, there will always eventually flash the bright creature you seek, however small. You must seize him and, by honoring him with action, make him grow and multiply. You can do it, and only you can do it.

Throughout all literature the voice of the Principle can be heard. For my final lines, my last celebration of the Principle, I turn to Hamlet, that eminent psychologist, who said:

> Refrain tonight,
> And that shall lend a kind of easiness
> To the next abstinence, the next more easy:
> For use almost can change the stamp of nature.